The
Responsible
Leader

The Responsible Leader

Developing a culture of responsibility in an uncertain world

Tim Richardson

KoganPage

LONDON PHILADELPHIA NEW DELHI

First published in Great Britain and the United States in 2015 by Kogan Page Limited

2nd Floor, 45 Gee Street
London EC1V 3RS
United Kingdom
www.koganpage.com

1518 Walnut Street, Suite 11004
Philadelphia PA 19102
USA

737/23 Ansari Road
Daryaganj
New Delhi 110002
India

© Tim Richardson, 2015

The right of Tim Richardson to be identified as the author of this work has been asserted by him in accordance with the Copyright, Designs and Patents Act 1988.

The material from the Project Sunlight website on pages 157 and 158 is reproduced with kind permission of Unilever and group companies.

ISBN   978 0 7494 7181 1
E-ISBN   978 0 7494 7182 8

British Library Cataloguing-in-Publication Data

A CIP record for this book is available from the British Library.

Library of Congress Cataloging-in-Publication Data

Richardson, Tim, 1959–
   The responsible leader : developing a culture of responsibility in an uncertain world / Tim Richardson.
      pages cm
      ISBN 978-0-7494-7181-1 (paperback) – ISBN 978-0-7494-7182-8 (ebk)   1. Leadership.
2. Responsibility.   I. Title.
   HD57.7.R52125 2015
   658.4'092–dc23
                                                                                          2014043315

Typeset by Graphicraft Limited, Hong Kong
Print production managed by Jellyfish
Printed and bound by CPI Group (UK) Ltd, Croydon CR0 4YY

CONTENTS

LIST OF FIGURES

FOREWORD

'The responsible leader' is exemplified by the author himself, whom I first met several years ago when he was a young and highly talented Director of Leadership Development at PwC. While Tim was helping shape fresh thinking within that organization, it became clear that his lateral and in-depth thinking could be equally useful serving a wider audience.

At the time, in the days leading up to the global financial crisis of 2008, Tim had spotted what was really going on, noticing both the symptoms and the causes of a potential malaise. He felt called to be something of a prophet in the wilderness.

His work since then, across the sectors and allied to his writings, has been helpful to all those endeavouring to make sense of their personal and working lives in increasingly challenging and demanding days.

Using a series of well-chosen case studies and personal experiences, Tim delineates not only how readily the alert responsible leader can detect shortcomings in a team or organization but also how vital and enriching a personal example of courageous authentic leadership, in life as in work, can be.

The progressive chapters of *The Responsible Leader* draw the reader inwards, towards self-examination, and then outwards and onwards towards practical suggestions as to how best to prepare oneself for demanding yet exciting lives of responsible leadership in the corporate or not-for-profit sectors or in the best of cases both.

In this way the responsible leader will be happy to raise the bar, to set standards and on occasions to stand alone not least in those knee-knocking moments of personal courage and decision-making.

Indeed through his own working life and experience, Tim has seen a whole host of managers doing things right but fewer genuine leaders who do the right thing. This book is a personal and at times almost spiritual call to the colours of being who you are as a responsible leader in recognising that everyone in your team or organization is, after all, someone else's child and as such warrants respect.

One can almost hear Tim speak as he writes – perhaps this is one of his greatest gifts – all the while encouraging us to be all that we can be and to see what a difference our lives of responsible leadership can and will make to all those in our charge and care.

Real lasting change happens one on one, one by one and then in partnerships. Facing this is ultimately both the task and the privilege of the responsible leader the foundation of whose life and leadership, as Tim portrays it, is grounded in the unselfish service of others. In times such as these, this is a message that will prove difficult for many to embrace but is surely needed.

Professor Norman Drummond CBE FRSE
Founder and Chairman
Columba 1400 and Drummond International

ACKNOWLEDGEMENTS

Inevitably with a book that has emerged over many years there are countless people that have been part of the exploration and aided the discovery. In some instances their contribution has been pivotal; in most cases small examples of responsible leadership in practice, unbeknown to them, have enriched my experience and the narrative. To those myriads of 'extras', I say a huge thank you.

Throughout the book I have mentioned some people by name (and occasionally changed the names for a variety of reasons) and I am deeply grateful for the time given to me during interviews and for the inspirational stories I have been able to use. Even as I write this acknowledgement, more people come to mind whom I would have liked to have featured and probably should have. I will continue to be on the lookout for role models and mention them as I tell the responsible leadership story.

Specifically, however, I do want to express my gratitude to a few individuals who have been with me along this journey. Thank you to Ralf Schneider, John Hughes, Hilary Farrar, Rosie Walford, Andrew Hollas, Martin Kalungu Banda and Anna Eliatamby who were all there when the experiential elements of responsible leadership in Africa and elsewhere evolved into more robust thinking.

A special thank you to Lorenza Clifford and Chris Neighbour for experimenting with this around the world with me and shaping models and frameworks along the way.

To my colleagues at Waverley – Chris Blakeley, Guy Rothwell and Belinda Smith in particular – your insights and encouragement have been invaluable. To Dr Karen Blakeley at Winchester, I have greatly appreciated your passion and energy, and I look forward to the unfolding story. To Dr Sharon Turnbull and Mike King from The Leadership Trust, I want to gratefully acknowledge your support in the early years and subsequently, and for your encouragement to write this book.

A special thank you to Professor Charles Handy who over many decades has written about this whole domain and challenged countless leaders to evaluate the what, the why and the how. These challenges have shaped my thinking. The personal challenge laid down from Charles Handy to me to continue to hold up the mirror to leaders inspired me to press on knowing that however small my contribution, it will have an impact.

I would like to express my deep appreciation to two mentors of mine: Norman Drummond, who kindly agreed to contribute a foreword and who models responsible leadership humbly, and Dr Nick Isbister, who reaffirms my strengths consistently.

To the editorial team at my publishers Kogan Page, I specifically want to thank you for the initial belief in the project and the ongoing reassurance, advice and technical insights that have resulted in a work that I am very pleased with.

Finally, a work of this kind takes time and commitment, and not a small amount of additional research and editing. My wife Caroline has been an ever-present sounding board and researcher spending countless hours editing and advising. Without her encouragement the writing process would have been far less rewarding and the finished product would have been incomplete.

Introduction

This is a book about ego, greed, betrayal, redemption and hopefulness. Ingredients, one might think, for a novel, but in this case the characters are real and the storylines are genuine. It is also a book about you and me, and the part we play in our own unique contexts. I do not want this book to be an exercise in talking 'about' leadership. That is easy and requires little investment on our part. Rather, I want to encourage each of us as players to pause and consider our response, first to the overarching question 'How can we lead responsibly and re-engage people's trust and respect as leaders?' and thereafter to a number of supplementary questions.

My intention in writing this book is first to raise your awareness of and attention to leaders and leadership as we experience them today. Secondly, I want to provoke challenge to our established thinking before offering some practical responses that individuals and organizations can take to evolve and be aligned with wider expectations of leadership in our fast-changing world.

As someone who has spent the past 25 years working with people and businesses – large and small, local and international – to help them grow and be effective, I am not interested in a purely academic text as I recognize in myself a fundamental drive to make a difference and see insights applied to real situations. Therefore this book is a blend – a helpful one, I hope – of theoretical positions and application ideas, often presented in the form of questions to prompt thinking. I have also highlighted throughout some case studies and examples that I believe illustrate the key points. That said, these examples are not all drawn from big business, as you might imagine. Given where we are with leadership (which we will explore shortly), it seems to me that we may need to look further afield for positive examples and role models. Indeed, this is itself one hallmark of responsible leadership, the willingness and ability to see beyond the obvious. But more of that later.

Flow of this book

In Chapter 1, I set out where we are currently and offer a challenge to notice and question what we can and should be observing about leaders and leadership. It is an opening statement of my and many others' view about what is right and, probably more importantly, what is wrong just now. I also want to set out what I believe are some dramatic forces that are at work in our world at the moment and that have an inevitable impact on how individuals can and should lead themselves and their organizations.

In Part 1, I will seek to set out a different paradigm for the future – the case for responsible leadership – and what this means for individuals and organizations. We will explore what distinguishes responsible leaders – the mindsets needed, which in turn shape behaviours – while acknowledging the dilemmas presented if we choose to go this way. We will also present a simple systemic model representing responsible leadership in action.

In Part 2, I will focus on how businesses and other organizations can and do go about developing a culture of responsibility and how this translates into developing individual responsible leaders. Although this might sound straightforward, there are traps and difficulties along the way. First and foremost, I intend to present a frank and honest picture and, where I have from my experience identified real challenges to overcome, I shall tell it as it is. After all, if this were easy we would all be doing it by now.

Throughout the book, in the form of 'reflections', I will provide some discussion questions and prompts that can be used individually and also in groups as you wish. My intent with these is to help you grapple with this emerging scenario and your response to it. The easy option will be to skim over these and move quickly on to the next chapter or section. If you find yourself doing this, I encourage you to pause momentarily to ask yourself why. Is it because you know the answers or that you have moved beyond this point in your own demonstration of leadership? That is quite possible, but so too is the fact that the point is challenging and might require your attention.

Finally, I want to end on a hopeful note, setting out a positive vision of the future for us to aspire towards (Part 3). I believe profoundly in the power of a positive narrative to inspire and call forth the good in us, so this book is not merely identifying a 'burning platform' (a phrase I have come to loathe in my time working with organizations, if I am totally honest).

As to a definition of responsible leadership, in Chapter 1 I set out what I believe to be the components of a definition that each of us can weigh in our contexts. What it does and will include is how we as leaders are more considerate, trustworthy, inspiring, interconnected, selfless and properly courageous. If you find yourself railing against these words, please read on. You may be surprised. If you find yourself agreeing with them, I am glad, and I invite you to press on too so that you may find encouragement.

Who is this book for?

Fundamentally, this book is for anyone who wants to think about leaders and leadership in the 21st century. There are many fabulous books available for those interested in leadership and I will reference many of these through-out. My perspective is one among many and I encourage you to have an open mind and to pick out nuggets that seem to resonate for you.

You may already be in a leadership position (senior or junior) in a large or small organization. Equally, you may be someone who aspires to be in a leadership position. Whether you have been doing this for some time or have been recently identified as someone with potential, I believe there is learning available, and my hope is that in this book you will find some that works for you.

For those working in the human resources (HR) or learning and develop-ment (L&D) or organizational development (OD) functions inside businesses, this book will provide you with some ideas and possible ammunition in your role. I have chosen to identify openly with this population as it is in this space that I have spent a large part of my working life. For ours is the task of influence and counsel, which itself carries great responsibility, perhaps without the overt recognition that comes with being the main man or woman.

As you read this book, you will inevitably have questions yourself. You will agree and disagree with me. You will cheer and be incensed. Naturally, I hope you enjoy it. Whatever your reaction or response, please engage with me in the debate and play your part in co-creating a different future. At the end of the book, I will offer some ways in which we can do this, together – another key principle of responsible leadership.

How did we end up here?

> *Only a few find the way; some don't recognize it when they do; some don't ever want to.*
> **(THE CHESHIRE CAT, ALICE IN WONDERLAND BY LEWIS CARROLL)**

To arrive at a shared understanding of what we mean by responsible leadership, I want to invite you to think upon the following set of words. What comes to mind and what images form for you when you read 'betrayal', 'mistrust', 'broken promises', 'feathering their own nests'? Now I invite you to do the same but for the following set of words: 'focused on the bigger picture', 'inspiring commitment', 'visionary', 'enabling'. You may have visualized people from the pages and screens of today's press or media. Perhaps a businessman. Perhaps a political leader. Maybe you found yourself drawing on characters or storylines from fiction or the movies. Equally, you may not have focused on people at all but found yourself generating other images from art or nature. I wonder if you thought about yourself or close friends and colleagues as you pondered on these simple words? Now consider the following phrases and what images they stimulate for you: 'concerned about the wider impact'; 'driven by something deeper'; 'bringing people together'; 'humble and determined'; 'brings the best out of people'. Such phrases could have been taken from a statement of capabilities for leaders and I have little doubt that they appear in many such frameworks. This book is about them and more. It is also about the less attractive words in the first sentence. This book is about leading differently, and to do that, you and I will need to consider how we *do* experience leadership, how we *would want to* experience leadership, and what the world today *needs* in the form of leadership.

The last point is critical. Our world is fast changing, more obviously interconnected than ever before, more diverse and full of apparent dilemmas and tensions. Tensions such as how to embrace both short-term and longer-term perspectives; how to steward resources wisely while providing for immediate basic needs; how to encourage use of talent and rewarding careers while preserving family units; how to reward investors while satisfying all stakeholders; how to respond with agility and behave ethically; how to be mindful of the needs of emerging and mature economies. Therefore, those who choose or are chosen to lead have this as their backdrop.

This book is about leading and being responsible, which is an orientation, an attitude, a way of being. It embraces:

- seeing the wider system or bigger picture and being intentionally mindful of the consequences of decisions in that wider system;
- choosing to be morally accountable and to act for the greater good in the short and long term;
- caring about others and enabling them to create;
- as a leader and as an organization, cultivating the right environment to make this possible.

My assertion is that this requires a fresh expression of leadership that is genuinely attractive to many and that benefits the many. One that is both simple and tough. The question, then, is what might this look like in practice and how can it be developed? Furthermore, who among us is ready to model it? We will address these questions throughout the book, but beforehand, it is helpful to contextualize our current situation by exploring the journey of discovery we have been on to understand leadership.

Forming our mental models of leadership

To begin with, we acknowledge that we have all constructed our mental models about leadership based on those people we have encountered in our lives who modelled leadership for us. Typically this happens first in those institutions we are part of early in our lives, such as schools, churches, communities, social and friendship groups, families even. Inspirational teachers and youth leaders can live with us for the rest of our lives. Equally so, the experience of bullies or dominant figures.

From the outset, as we all have a strong drive to belong, to fit in, and as we learn by mimicking, it is no surprise that we try to replicate those behaviours and patterns that we see in people whom we regard as being effective or impressive. Thus our personal perspectives on leading and being led are shaped.

Allow me a short personal story to illustrate this and maybe spark a connection for you. When I was at secondary school at the formative ages of

11 through 16, I was exposed to leadership at its most raw. The headmaster of the grammar school I attended was at the top of the hierarchy. He was first an academic and an archaeologist. He was passionate about history and took delight in encouraging his pupils to explore history kinaesthetically – an inspiration to anyone who loved history, naturally.

He was charged primarily with the direction and management of a school containing seven hundred boys and the potent mix of testosterone, ambition and mischief. He had authority and was respected, which was made easier because he was a cheerful man who did his best to connect with pupils. He had power through his position in the system. As Barry Oshry identified in his insightful work on systems thinking (2007), to which we will refer periodically in this book, he was the 'top'. I represented the bottom of this particular system. He and his fellow teachers could use their power to inspire, encourage and release. Equally, they could use it to suppress and sow fear.

Within the different levels in the school system, leadership was demonstrated in many different ways and informally. Class clowns led through personality. Gifted sports people led through their ability to galvanize and achieve. Subject-matter experts led through their knowledge and, if they were skilled enough, their ability to share that with others. School bullies tried to lead by control and fear. Emergent leadership was recognized as pupils were invited to take on responsibility as prefects and monitors – the historical Greek and Roman influences were strong, and, for one of them, the prize of being head boy. Unfortunately, the bases for these selections were not communicated, which, upon reflection, I think was a missed opportunity. But then it was the mid-1970s and our understanding of leadership effectiveness as a society was embryonic.

What has all this got to do with our topic of 'the responsible leader' and moreover leadership as we experience it today? First, I want to encourage you to adopt a thoughtful and reflective approach, and by illustrating leadership from an experience that we can all relate to, we begin to bring our own perspective front of mind.

In a school, a remarkably full gambit of leadership manifestations is present, and much of it is to do with human nature and our natural responses and reactions. This will manifest through our natural instinct to follow and conform in order to belong, or our natural instinct to influence and control. It will involve our unavoidable urge to be with people who are like us. Through these reactions and responses we develop patterns of thinking that shape how we lead and follow. And these patterns are tested, verified, challenged and reshaped along life's journey.

Reflections

- Who has shaped your mental models of leadership and how?

- How have you challenged these personal mental models, if at all?

Leadership through the ages

Before delving more deeply into what we might mean by responsible leadership and the role of the responsible leader specifically, it is helpful to place this into the context of a timeline of leadership thinking and insight.

Leadership has been around since the dawning of time and is present in every shape of human community, society or grouping. Early civilizations across the globe, biblical accounts, historical records and commentators all identify rulers, military champions and commanders, bishops, mystics, elders and the like who have exercised power over others. However, it was the hunger for growth, development and advantage (often economic or imperial) in the 19th and 20th centuries that drove scholars to study leaders and leadership in earnest in order to look for threads and patterns. Thereafter, countless definitions of leadership emerged, theories developed, thousands upon thousands of books were written (I appreciate that this is yet another one and the irony is not lost on me), all with the intention, presumably, of trying to unpick one of humankind's fundamental behaviour traits, namely that we have an inclination to want to be led by others and to follow, choosing to do so by and large as an act of our will.

I appreciate fully that humankind's history is riddled with accounts of coercion and manipulation of the most horrendous kind by leaders. The psychology of followership and choice is a whole study in itself and one that I shall not delve into too deeply here. I will reference followers and followership as this book develops, largely from the standpoint of people taking personal responsibility for their choices both as leaders and followers.

As scholars have dissected leaders and leadership, we have encountered, perhaps discovered, a number of distinct theoretical models. The military model was probably the first to be identified and is perhaps the easiest to appreciate, despite the fact that many of us have no experience of being in the military. Typically referred to as *command and control*, this model describes a formal hierarchy based on status and position in which senior people make decisions and pass down instructions to subordinates, relying on officer structures to execute orders and a system of rules (and consequences) to enforce compliance. If this sounds out of date to you, I encourage you to think again, as we will see shortly as we reflect on recent incidents of great and disappointing leadership. My grammar school operated with this model clearly in evidence. Indeed, without it, goodness knows what might have happened!

As thinkers explored leaders and leadership, it became clear that there could be merit in identifying traits and characteristics that (presumably) effective leaders possessed. Clearly, if it were possible to identify these, society could identify people who had them and used them, thereby accelerating leaders into important positions. This paved the way for vast numbers of theories, tools, techniques and institutions dedicated to developing and teaching leadership. These exist today and are, as a sweeping generalization, mostly helpful.

A question arose, naturally. Could leadership be taught or was it genetic? After all, some people are natural born leaders, yes?

The role of charisma

A more vexing question it has been hard to imagine in this field. As we saw in school, charisma played a huge part in informal leaders emerging. And to this day, many people believe in the charisma model. We need look no further than the election of the Mayor of London for a contemporary example. Boris Johnson became Mayor in 2008 and is a colourful character with considerable charisma. Blessed with a powerful intellect and a quick wit, he won the popular vote. He connects with people. He also infuriates many. Although he was not Mayor of London at the time it was granted the 2012 Olympic Games (in 2005), he is acknowledged as being a key factor in making the London Games successful through his strength of personality and willingness to be seen to be at the helm.

Whether we like it or not, charisma will not go away. I have met many successful and unsuccessful leaders, both in business and elsewhere, with generous helpings of natural charisma. Some are skilful in their ability to handle it (Boris Johnson is clearly one such) and some sadly not. As human beings we tend to be drawn to charisma. Unfortunately for charismatic leaders, we can also be all too ready to drop them, as many a politician will testify throughout the centuries. But the questions remain: Can you teach leadership? Can you teach or develop charisma? Should you?

Situational leadership

During my teenage years my good friend Jeremy was a technical wizard. Jeremy liked nothing better than dismantling things, finding out how they worked and reassembling them. He was the man in charge of the sound desk for the band. He was a technical expert and as such was the leader at critical times when no one else knew what was needed. Situationally he stepped up to lead when required. Successfully erecting a tent for the scouts was down to Jeremy.

It was Paul Hersey and Ken Blanchard (1969) who popularized 'situational leadership' as a distinct theory in which the right approach to and style of leadership is dependent on the task at hand and the maturity of the people to lead. Clearly, 'situations' have been around since time began, so the identifying and naming of what Hersey and Blanchard observed to be effective was just that, a discovery of something that works. In the quest for proving whether leadership could be taught they revealed one key truth, namely that leaders who seemed to read the situation and the people could adapt their style appropriately or find someone who was better equipped for that specific occasion. Moreover, this could be taught and guidance given to aspirant and existing leaders.

Further interpretations

Over the decades, as scholars have studied individuals and organizations (predominantly successful ones, it should be said) for patterns and secrets, we have begun to notice approaches that it is possible to analyse and emulate. We have noticed that some leaders seem more able to connect deeply and resonate with the groups and people they lead (Boyatzis and McKee, 2005). We have seen that people tend to follow and respond to individuals who appear authentic and naturally at ease within themselves and with their role. For some, the fact that a leader leads from principles or with tough love is attractive (Goffee and Jones, 2006). For others, it is the presence of tough humility that works best (Collins, 2001). Servant leadership (Greenleaf, 1998) has been seen to be both effective and attractive, but so too has been the strength and charisma of leaders who lead in the sporting arena and typically lead from the front or by example. Given this myriad of theories, what are we to believe? How should we respond? Is there a right way or best way?

It was clear that in my grammar school many different forms of leadership were operating simultaneously and that the organization itself both allowed it and functioned effectively. Even today, 40 years later, schools will function effectively when some degree of command and control is exercised along-side teachers who can connect and engage inspirationally with their pupils.

In the Industrial Revolution of the 18th century, many organizations and businesses formed around the need to produce things consistently, uniformly and in large quantities. People were not used to working this way (as agriculture is a quite different structure) and factory managers managed and led presumably in the only ways they knew how, drawn from the military and religion – command and control. Organized education emerged along the same lines. Power was vested in position and status. But times change. To spare the in-depth history lesson, let's come right up to date with what we notice now.

Changes in sources of power: a 21st-century revolution

Simply put, we are in the midst of another revolution, and it is having a profound impact on our understanding of leadership, and what we are looking for in those who choose to lead us. This revolution is affecting everyone on the planet and in many ways simultaneously. Think about that for a moment. It has probably never happened before in the history of mankind.

Let's try and unpick this phenomenon by looking at some themes that we notice when we pause and think about it.

Information overload

First, it's about technological advancements that are creating previously un-thinkable levels of access to information. The internet has enabled traders in New York, London, Hong Kong, Sydney and São Paolo to deal in the blink of an eye and if they wanted to, Masai warriors on the African plains could do likewise. There may not be plumbed-in running water, but through wireless communication a tribesman or woman has access to the internet and all the riches and potential of limitless information. In the developed world we now have so much information available to us that many are finding it difficult to cope. Stress levels at work are increasing in many western countries and, far from the new leisure age bringing us happiness, many countries now report increasing levels of depression and unhappiness in the quest to acquire knowledge, master it and perform at impossibly high levels all the time. Suicide rates among the younger generations in South Korea, for example, have increased suddenly over the past ten years under the apparent pressure to study and perform academically.

Up until the late 20th century, knowledge and information were controllable. Academic institutions by and large held knowledge and passed it on. Information was held by state institutions or the media. More importantly, the choice of what information was available was down to 'them'. Suddenly, this is no longer the case. Individual people can now post and upload information, news, comments and research, all with minimal controls. Wikipedia is one example of the age of mass participation in sharing information and knowledge and I suspect that not a single school teacher in the western world exists who has not had to mark a piece of homework cut and pasted directly from Wikipedia.

Wikileaks is now the scourge of politicians, security establishments and people in the public eye. YouTube has opened up a veritable Pandora's box of opportunity for sharing the good, the bad and, sadly, the ugly. You might be asking what this has got to do with leadership and the revolution I mentioned earlier.

At the time of writing, the United Nations is grappling with what to do about the unfolding catastrophe in Syria and in particular a response to an alleged attack by the ruling powers on its own people, using chemical weapons. Much of the supposed evidence is in the form of amateur video footage posted on YouTube and the internet by people experiencing the events first hand. World leaders must now deliberate as to what information is trustworthy and what is not. And woe betide anyone who hesitates, because this revolution sweeping the world is rapid. Our expectation levels have changed to the extent that we now demand news and data instantly and, with that, the corresponding decisions. The adage (attributed rightly or wrongly to Harold Wilson and much used by subsequent politicians) that 'a week in politics is a long time' has never been more true. A day perhaps would be more accurate.

So we can see that technology invented 'for everyone' really is impacting everyone (Sir Tim Berners-Lee, the inventor of the internet, famously said that 'this is for everyone'). News happening anywhere around the world is instantly available everywhere. Imagine, therefore, as a leader of a global business, for example, the pressure that this might exert on you to be fully up to speed all the time. Your company decisions rely on this.

If you think that this phenomenon is only relevant for large organizations or political leaders, think again. Someone running a small charity that provides learning activities for young people using the outdoors now has to monitor whether individuals are taking videos without permission and posting them who knows where. Schools now have to consider how to embrace and manage access to the internet for their students on site and off.

Multiple stakeholders demanding to be heard

Secondly, the whole question of who are relevant stakeholders has changed and continues to change. Historically, for example, a company focused on delivering value to its owners (possibly shareholders) through the sale of goods or services at a profit to customers. Simple. Not anymore. Certainly the same fundamental objective holds true, but nowadays so many more parties are interested in the story. Because of the rapid dissemination of information globally, more individual customers and suppliers have the ability to comment on and raise issues that previously would have been dealt with out of public scrutiny. The general public is sucked into the mix and has begun to exert power through boycotting or championing products or particular businesses. Take Starbucks, for example – a proud company simply providing coffee around the world and doing some excellent work with communities globally (more of this later). Then it becomes public knowledge that it has been clever about its tax policies, in the UK in particular. As is well documented, it has operated entirely within the fiscal regimes operating in Europe and yet through the power of the social media combining with the formal media (and a political establishment desperate for something to please the crowd), the company found itself in the modern-day equivalent of the village stocks being pelted with rotten vegetables. Whether the company liked it or not, the crowd had decided on perceived guilt or perhaps just on being far too clever for people to understand. The result: public anger and boycotting of coffee shops. It remains to be seen how the business deals with this in the future. Will it change its approach and policies? And it will call for some courageous and possibly different leadership, as we will see later.

Clarity around who a business's stakeholders actually are is now hard. The picture is blurred and dealing with blurriness has become an important criterion for leaders both in the commercial and in the public sector. Local authorities in the UK have now been audited in public by the public, often with good reason, and unsuspecting civil servants have typically been caught out. The need to identify and manage complex stakeholders is a key requirement for future leaders.

Distinct generations all alive at once

As we consider the concept of stakeholders, we must also note that this revolutionary phenomenon is being experienced by clearly defined generations all at the same time and all with different expectations and experiences of it. Recently I was in a meeting in a large organization at which were present four clearly delineated generations. I was part of a group that represented the Baby Boomers, born as I was in 1959 just before the 1960s times of never having had it so good. Also present in the room were people who represented Generation X – individuals in their late 30s and early 40s, two people who were in their mid-20s and are categorized as Generation Y, and an intern born in 1995 who would now be regarded as Generation Z. The subject matter of the meeting is not important. What was fascinating was to observe the different approaches taken to communication, to attention, to language and to the fundamentals of human interaction. You may assume that the latter two generations, Y and Z, would have limited attention spans and patience. Perhaps that they would be disrespectful and easily bored? Interestingly, they may have been, but it was also acutely apparent that the Baby Boomers and Generation X were the ones struggling to focus and deal with too many interruptions (via Blackberry devices and the like). Whether modern-day leaders can embrace fully and openly the tensions this brings will be an important question. Many will try to judge or take entrenched views. Most likely this will not demonstrate the necessary inclusiveness now demanded by all these different generational groups.

Employees' voice and the change in the employment contract

Since the turn of the century, larger organizations especially have come under pressure from another source, this time internally. But it didn't start there. The Industrial Revolution brought with it horrendous working conditions and exploitation of workers in the quest for production. For the most part, this is not disputed. It was also the seedbed for the emergence of perhaps the earliest examples of responsible leaders, many of whom were industrialists and entrepreneurs who saw the benefit and wisdom in treating their employees decently, humanely and fairly. A good number of these were motivated by a sense of personal value and a higher calling, and indeed many were Quakers. In her excellent book *Chocolate Wars* Deborah Cadbury charts the history of chocolate, which was also the story of Quaker business families who modelled employee engagement well before it became a buzzword of the 21st century (2010). Deborah Cadbury is herself descended from the Cadbury family and writes with genuine insight mixed with a clear sense of responsibility and emotional connection about the rise of the Cadbury brand, what it stands for and what it has now become. The book is both a historical text and a wonderful story of intrigue, ingenuity, innovation, love and warmth.

It could be argued that what has happened recently has been the combination of a number of forces. First, technological advances enable views to be shared instantly and widely. These views will include the fact that, generationally, expectations from a career and life have evolved such that many Gen Y and Gen Z now regard working for many different organizations in their early years as an essential route to take. Two years in a role is now a long time. Older generations and younger ones alike are now demanding that the employer–employee contract is changed. The notion of employers having to think creatively about their employee value proposition is very present. When McKinsey coined its now famous phrase 'the war for talent' (Michaels, Handfield-Jones and Axelrod, 1997), it was the first that many corporate leaders had heard about how they should think more purposefully about what they do to attract and keep the people who will deliver real value and strategic advantage. They identified that growth would be dependent on a business's ability to attract people in the midst of an over-demand for limited talent, largely, it should be said, in the dotcom era. Many commentators now believe that a new war for talent is upon us, one that is driven by the need to attract the *right* talent to meet known and unknown needs. It is not unusual now for large businesses to have to embrace human resources practices such as career breaks, maternity and paternity leave, part-time working and home working/virtual working. Furthermore, it is no longer acceptable for an employer to ignore demands for a rewarding career and fulfilling work–life balanced with a life outside work.

Access to news and mass media promulgates views on what makes for a rewarding life and career, and this shapes responses. Recently, a young intern at a global bank based in London was found dead in his shower having to all intents and purposes exhausted himself through a 'long hours' culture and presenteeism, doing what he thought was *expected* of him. Public shock forced the bank in question to take a deep and long look at their apparently Dickensian culture and practices. Such incidents will increasingly play on the minds of senior leaders and HR departments, and rightfully so.

The globalization revolution

Quite when the term globalization emerged is unclear. Mankind has traded across borders for hundreds of years on foot, on horseback and via the oceans. So it can hardly be a new phenomenon. Labour has moved around the globe over the centuries, both voluntarily and forcibly. Capital movement and accessibility is a more recent development and yet we are still talking about globalization as a major force both for change and for uncertainty. It follows that there must be some other aspects at work.

We can certainly confirm that many more businesses are now owned outside their original national boundaries, from banks to utility companies, from car manufacturing to clothing. Naturally, this brings with it issues of culture and business practices. Can they or should they be uniform? Is leading a business in the United States the same as leading a business in Japan? What if it is the same business? Are stakeholders' expectations the same around the globe?

Banking is one sector grappling with this very issue. Consider for example how HSBC, one of the largest banking groups in the world, has been endeavouring to create what it has branded 'The World's Local Bank' (this has been its strapline for many years), with operations in every continent. Having recently spent time working with this organization as one of my clients, I can testify to the complexity of this task and that culturally and operationally, banking across the globe is both the same and different. We will return to this theme later as well.

Perhaps, though, a key aspect of modern-day globalization is that, returning to our earlier theme of stakeholders, citizens around the world are now so much more aware of everything that is happening around the world and with that comes expectations of fairness, interpretations of justice and trust, product compatibility, pricing and taxation policies; the list goes on. Once we add to that the forces of global environmentalism and movements such as those formed to eradicate global poverty, we can begin to see that it is more than just an issue of trade nowadays.

By way of a final point in the globalization discussion, it is worth a word or two about resources and resource allocation. Basic economic theory teaches us that scarcity is the enemy of demand and the friend of the profiteer. Given a global population set to increase by 40 per cent over the next 40 years, mostly in the developing countries of Africa, South America and South Asia, it does not take a genius to work out that resources fundamental to our human existence and well-being, such as energy, water, food and minerals for construction, are going to be the focus of attention. Such attention either will be negative and manifest as disputes, sharp trade practices, unjust distribution and perhaps even wars, or there is the potential for positive ways forward as mankind's ingenuity and collaboration seek to find creative solutions to dilemmas. Either way, the future is not going to be easy to predict.

Relationships and structures: when hierarchy prevents action

As we saw, a school has a clearly defined structure and hierarchy that generally works. In the same way, a Navy ship or submarine functions effectively when each crew member knows his or her role and can execute instructions knowing that there is accountability throughout the vessel. During the Korean War, my father served on board a large Royal Navy aircraft carrier on which two separate operations were present: the ship itself, with all the means to move it around the world, alongside the structures and command needed to fly aircraft effectively and safely. Hearing him tell of accidentally finding himself on the flight deck during an intense time of take-offs and landings was one of my fondest stories from his wartime experience. The point is that, in this example, we can see that there was (and continues to be) a need to balance differing models and differing pressures within one system. Decision-making in this environment is tightly controlled – and needs to be. Often it is vested at the top level in one person (or a very small group) who typically cascades instructions through the chain of command. Individuals further down the hierarchy know and fully understand that their duty is to act upon these instructions unquestionably.

Now, as we have begun to see, even the world of the military is changing. Recently, I was speaking to someone who told me that his brother worked in Las Vegas. When I asked what he did there, I was expecting a response such as croupier or hotel manager. What I did not expect was to be advised that he worked for the British Army and that he fought wars from the middle of the desert using drone planes. It transpired that he controlled these remotely from thousands of miles away, using information gleaned on the ground and from satellites. Amazing. My paradigms and assumptions about military operations were felled in one moment because technology has allowed us to do things very differently. One man in the desert thousands of miles away is fighting a war by precisely selecting a target from a screen. (I fully appreciate the controversy that rages over drone operations and strikes around the world. I neither condone nor condemn them myself. I merely use this story to illustrate a point about the changing nature of structures and the need for leadership to adapt rapidly.)

In the same way, new organizations are emerging that are challenging organizational structures. When Google began in 1998, Larry Page and Sergy Brin began it from Stanford University and a friend's garage. Having reframed internet searching through their remarkable algorithm, the business simply reinvented the role of information in the world. The emergence of

Google Maps, Google Earth and Android, to name but a few developments, has changed the way we live. Moreover, it has changed the way we gather information and make decisions. As I write this book, I find myself 'googling' things (the verb to google has recently been added to our dictionaries) because I believe I can trust the source. Google is now a very large player on the global stage. In 2013 it was only 15 years old and its vital statistics read (as of 30 June 2013 – *Bloomberg BusinessWeek*):

- $290 billion in market cap;
- $56.6 billion in revenue reported in the last four quarters;
- 44,777 employees.

At the time of writing, Twitter is being considered for flotation with an estimated market value of $14 billion. This is a business that has emerged from nowhere, providing a platform for mass communication. As analysts struggle with how to value a business like this, what is clear is that old models involving revenues and profits from making or selling something of determined value are being challenged by the sheer momentum generated by the crowd that is signing up in their millions. Access to millions of stakeholders has now become the value of a business. Tesco, the giant UK-based retailer, realized this when it launched the now ubiquitous 'store loyalty card' in 1995. In seeking to provide great customer service, it stumbled across the value of holding data about its millions of customers down to the items they buy each week and how this can inform the store about the actual and potential buying patterns of you and me. So valuable is this kind of data that companies will pay huge sums for access to it. The market segment of 'one' has arrived. So at the same time as a huge database has value, we now see the phenomenon of a sales effort or promotion targeted directly to an individual customer.

Such businesses as Google and Twitter are examples of rapid growth into modern-day giants that are themselves challenging the established giants. For example, BT – the UK's flagship telecoms business – has found itself having to move into the pay-to-view sports coverage market packaged on the back of its broadband provision in order to protect revenues and maintain its customer base. Whether this courageous decision on the part of the new CEO Gavin Patterson to tackle the satellite broadcasters head-on pays off remains to be seen, but it represents one example of a senior leader willing to embrace change quickly and provoke a business that many thought sluggish and set in its ways to surprise customers and stakeholders.

However, this technological revolution continues to provide opportunities for start-ups and small businesses to play with the big boys. No longer do organizations need fixed office bases. In London where I live and in almost every other large commercial city, over the past 10 years or so, hubs have proliferated. Essentially a 'hub' is like a large common room or collection of common rooms in which small businesses gather to do their work and grow their businesses. Renting an office is often seen as either out of reach for these businesses on a cost basis or simply unnecessary. After all, with a mixed technology platform and some smart ideas I can reach the whole world now. Far better to hire small spaces, a desk or workstation, share other facilities and surround myself with like-minded, energetic entrepreneurs. Many such individuals testify to the sheer electricity of such hubs and how it has helped them incubate ideas and gain access to resources and even capital investments.

Whether this spells the end for the large corporation is probably premature, but it does mean that the kind of rules that operated for as long as anyone can remember will probably no longer apply. For example, entrants to markets can come from anywhere now, and whereas the cost of entry might have been prohibitive in the past, it is now entirely possible for one man or woman and a 3D printer to compete with larger manufacturing operations.

More important is the fact that traditional structures risk proving an encumbrance to speed of response. Hierarchical decision-making processes that safeguarded businesses now hold them back from competing and expose them to attacks from enterprises that can demonstrate portfolio agility and rapid innovation, often through collaboration and short-term tie-ups.

A final point about structure also helps inform our thinking about responsible leadership. If command and control structures and processes have limited use in many of today's more vibrant and emerging organizations, then how is leadership demonstrated? As we will see, enlightened leaders at the top of an organization are fast waking up to the fact that leadership is exercised at all levels in the system and often by people without formal leadership positions or authority. Recognizing this, allowing it, encouraging it and rewarding it will become more critical for the responsible leader rather than mandating, directing and controlling through outdated structures.

Drowning under regulation

The forces impacting leaders in business and other organizations are unrelenting and fast changing. No more so than in the world of regulation. I do not intend to go into this area in detail given that there are thousands of rules and regulations in place to govern the way business is done and organizations are run, and I for one am certainly not motivated to explore these. No, my angle on this is different. Regulation has increased both because of centralization (as in the European Union) to ensure a level playing field and maintain quality, *and* because governments and society at large have felt that businesses cannot be trusted to behave, as in the world of financial services where regulation has been necessary to protect customers and drive ethical standards of conduct. Whether either objective has been achieved is debatable. What is clear, though, is that for leaders of organizations, there is a constant scrutiny which itself exerts pressure, which some might relish but which is often received unhelpfully. By way of illustration and to remind us that this kind of revolution is not limited to commerce or banking, I was recently at a hospital in the UK where standards have slipped across some measures of effectiveness used in the National Health Service. I was brought in to begin to help leaders there find the motivation and techniques that can lift morale and model different behaviours. What was interesting, though, was the pressure, tangible in some places, that had been visited upon the organization by the various visits of the Care Quality Commission, which had felt like a beating by the head teacher. As the pace of change accelerates, it is hard to imagine governments relenting on regulation, and as businesses are increasingly globalizing their reach they will have to become adept at navigating regulations in different territories, perhaps even conflicting ones.

A final point: to consume or steward?

I mention this final point because the revolution that is sweeping the globe is also beginning to be a revolution of conscience and, to a degree, philosophical. As the 20th century closed and the 21st century opened, the driving force behind the global economy was consumerism. The West was already addicted to consumerism, racking up huge debts – governmentally and personally – to fuel an apparently insatiable appetite for goods and lifestyle. The East was (and is) developing the habit. China, once a predominantly agrarian economy, has been on a 50-year charge towards consumerism and industrialization. Huge metropolises have emerged from seemingly nowhere and the construction boom seems to know no bounds. Lifestyles and values have changed, leaving the country divided between traditionalists and progressive (often younger) generations. A visit to Hong Kong or Shanghai is now even more of an assault on the senses, as the pace of life in these cities is frantic.

Arab and Middle Eastern lands that for centuries have been slow-paced and often nomadic have sprinted into the future. In Dubai, it is now possible to view the world's tallest building from an artificial ski slope in the desert.

And yet all this unrelenting consumerism is beginning to be challenged by younger generations, some leading thinkers and, interestingly, some celebrity figures. Bono, the lead singer of U2, has for many years been leading a campaign to eradicate poverty and distribute wealth more equitably. Peter Block, the well-known business guru, has through his Abundant Communities Initiative been challenging the status quo around American consumerist culture by encouraging more communities to look inward to their own resources to meet needs – a return to bartering in many ways. Sir Tim Smit, through his remarkable Eden Project in Cornwall, has given thousands of people a vision of more sustainable land use and how to educate future generations about stewardship.

These few examples are just the tip of the iceberg as the revolution begins to challenge our thinking patterns. The economic crisis that reached its nadir in 2008 could be said to have been something of a clarion call. Indeed, the Occupy movement that sprang up shortly afterwards seemed to capture the public's imagination as pictures of tents camped outside St Paul's Cathedral went viral, as did their message of how the few were distorting the system against the many. Global capitals have seen their own Occupy demonstrations, perhaps another angle of globalization that the economists and politicians had not foreseen.

Such questioning has not found definitive answers as yet, but what is certainly clear is that it is not going to slow down or go away. Quite the opposite is more likely. And how this will impact on leaders of businesses, governments and charities is not certain, save for the fact that it will certainly impact decision-making and responses.

Summary

Forces driving a revolution:

- information overload;
- multiple stakeholders all wanting to be heard;
- distinct generations alive at once;
- relationships and structures: when hierarchy prevents action;
- employees' voice and the change in the employment contract;
- the globalization revolution;
- drowning under regulation;
- consumerism or stewardship.

We have overflown the landscape at a helicopter level, to use the management jargon. What we have begun to see is that our understanding of leadership is evolving and that it is changing, given some of the forces operating in our world today. The points we have covered about this revolution do not represent an exhaustive list. We have not addressed political forces, for example – who would dare to speculate there! What they illustrate is what some modern commentators have called the VUCA world – volatile, uncertain, complex, ambiguous (the concept of a VUCA world was introduced by the US military as the Cold War ended and as the United States looked out over the emergence of a multilateral, rather than a bilateral, global landscape) – and one in which leaders will be required to lead us. And this will require a fresh exploration of, and expression of, leadership – in my view, a more responsible paradigm.

Reflections

- As you read about forces affecting change in our world, which ones resonated most for you/your team/your business? Why? What others specific to you might you need to acknowledge?

- What is the nature of the leadership challenges that you face now and as you look into the future?

- To what extent are these old challenges that have resurfaced or repeated themselves, or are they new and not previously encountered?

- How do you feel about leadership as you look into the future, and importantly, how do you feel about your personal leadership?

PART ONE
A fresh response: outlining the case for responsible leadership

What distinguishes responsible leaders?

02

Why should anyone be led by you?

(ROB GOFFEE AND GARETH JONES)

Regulation alone cannot be sufficient to govern the market. We have to look deeply at important questions of purpose, ethos and responsibility.

(LORD GREEN, FORMER CHAIRMAN AND CEO OF HSBC)

In the VUCA (volatile, uncertain, complex, ambiguous) world where uncertainty prevails, we have a conundrum. How can we lead people in the traditional and expected ways when we do not know clearly what is going on? Will this work? How, if at all, do the ways we think about leaders and leadership need to evolve further? This part of the book sets out to build a more detailed picture of that fresh expression.

Initially, by way of a reminder, leadership theory over time identifies that effective leaders typically *do* the following (among other actions). They:

- have a clear vision for the future;
- set direction;
- inspire others to follow them;
- enable greatness in others;

- are able to mobilize teams and resources to deliver against that vision;
- create followership through trust, respect and loyalty, among other things.

The above are some of the answers that we often hear when we ask the question: 'What do great leaders do?'

When we ask the supplementary question about what qualities effective leaders possess, charisma plays a part, as we have seen, and is often evidenced by a kind of aura and presence. Talk to anyone who met Margaret Thatcher, Nelson Mandela or Bill Clinton and they will all agree that when these individuals came in to the room, the atmosphere changed, as if filled by their own magnetism. People were drawn to them. When you meet Richard Branson, founder and driving force behind the Virgin brand, you are struck first by the fact that he is not a large man (Clinton, like Mandela, is over six feet tall) but that he has a remarkable ability to make you feel special when he is talking to you, as he seems to focus exclusively on you. He is renowned for not being a typical businessman concentrating on numbers and performance but a leader who is an ideas generator and more of a people person, very much at home in a celebration and limelight launch.

These qualities are far from redundant in the modern world. Throughout time, when faced with journeys of fear and uncertainty, followers have tended to look for reassurance and confidence, someone in whom they can believe and someone in whom they can trust. As followers, we give our discretionary loyalty and commitment based on a wide range of factors, including the extent to which a leader commands our respect, earns our trust, wins our affection, inspires our response and action, and believes in us such that we believe in ourselves.

In the 21st century, when many leaders across all aspects of our lives – business, religion, politics, communities – have been found out for betraying trust and diminishing value, there is a call for leaders who exhibit strength of character that balances talent and capability. I invite you to join me in building a more complete picture of responsible leadership. In the previous chapter we identified that to lead responsibly is to have a wider systemic perspective and to be mindful of how decisions impact that system positively and for the greater good. Now I propose that we start by highlighting some foundational paradigms – patterns of thinking – that we should be looking for in our leaders of today and tomorrow. I believe in simplicity if at all possible. Figure 2.1 presents a simple progression and virtuous cycle that I have found helpful when working with individuals and groups – one that provides a

FIGURE 2.1   Responsible leadership: authentic core

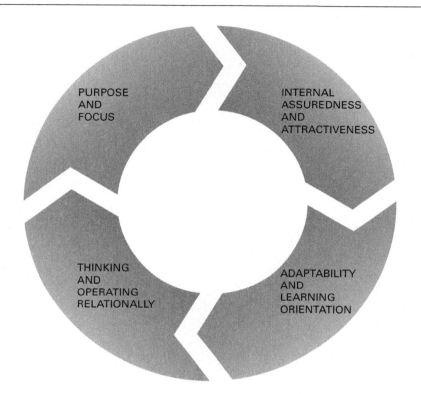

foundational understanding of important paradigms that is needed now and in the future in our leaders.

Simply and first, if my leadership is about how I reassure and inspire others to act, perform or achieve, we should consider what it is that will draw people to my leadership and what it is that encourages people to trust and respect me. Based on what we know about people who lead well now and most likely in the future, we can identify four important points at the core of being a responsible leader (Figure 2.2):

- the degree to which leaders possess and exude internal assuredness and attractiveness;

- the degree to which they are adaptable and oriented to learn;

- the degree to which they think and operate relationally;

- the degree to which they inspire others with their purpose and focus.

FIGURE 2.2   The role of internal assuredness and attractiveness

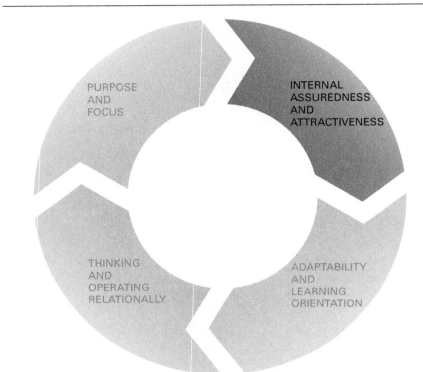

Internal assuredness and attractiveness

The starting point in this virtuous cycle is the fact that responsible leaders know who they are, are confident yet humble, and their authenticity is attractive (see Figure 2.2). The principle of attractiveness is an important one for responsible leaders, as this draws people to want to work with and be led by such leaders. By attractiveness, we are not referring to any physical appearance, but rather the natural presence that engages with others and appeals to others at a deeper emotional level.

In much of my work with leaders across all sectors I tend to ask the following questions, often early on in my interactions with them:

- Who are you?
- What do you stand for?
- Why should people follow you and trust you?
- How can you lead from your natural strengths?

I have worked with senior groups throughout the world who are often floored by such simple questions, expecting instead a session on the skills and qualities needed to be an effective leader. And yet, unless we are able to answer these fundamental questions, as Rob Goffee and Gareth Jones say in their great book *Why Should Anyone Be Led by You?* (2006), we present people with an unauthentic role model that is potentially confusing and not reassuring.

What does this mean and look like in practice?

Clarity about identity

At the core of the responsible leader is a quiet assuredness based on a clear sense of 'who I am'. A strong personal identity, if you will. This is built on a **real understanding and acceptance of one's uniqueness – personality, motivations, strengths and weaknesses** – and a confidence that means 'I do not need to pretend to be someone I am not'. For example, Richard Branson is not a gifted public speaker. I have seen and heard him and it is quite painful to watch. But he knows this and does not let this weakness hinder his personal effectiveness, which is based on his ability to see an opportunity, his drive to prove others wrong, his sense of adventure, his strong sense of justice and freedom, and his love of people and belief in their potential. These are what make him unique and attractive to millions of people, customers and staff alike.

I work with many individuals, helping them explore their personal story as they reflect back through their lives to discover the patterns they intuitively follow that reveal what drives them and what gives them real and deep fulfilment. To be 'in the flow', in the words of Mihály Csíkszentmihályi (2002), is to be so absorbed and focused as to feel that one is operating almost effortlessly. And this is very powerful, both for the individual *and* for those observing. I recently sat in a lecture theatre listening to a professor from a London university talking to teenagers who might be prospective students at a brand new school. His talk was about how engineering and biology were becoming interlinked, resulting in the development of new technologies that were just astonishing. However, what was even more impressive to me was his passion and natural ability to communicate his subject with wit and in a way that was simply compelling. He was 'in his element' as Ken Robinson would say (2009). Robinson (himself a truly gifted communicator) expands on the profound truth that when as humans we are operating in our element – doing what we seemingly were made to do – it is wonderful to behold. As such, the professor was inspiring both to me as an adult and moreover to the assembled 14- and 15-year-olds. I was not surprised to find out that he was a regular presenter on TV as well.

Being clear about these aspects of one's identity allows a leader to relax and get on with leading – making decisions, inspiring others, mobilizing resources.

Clarity about personal values

The next step towards internal assuredness is **being clear about personal values and beliefs and living by these**. Although there is nothing new in this, I am amazed at the number of people in senior leadership positions who have never taken the time to pause, reflect, and dig deep to find out what they stand for. I am talking about much more here than the corporate blandness surrounding values statements such as 'honesty, integrity and teamwork' (apologies if these are your company's values – they happen to be the three most popular values words used by corporations). I am talking about beliefs, morals and ethics. For it is these that actually govern behaviours and the choices we make. We can get quite specific here, too. By way of example, I heard a debate on the radio after the tragic suicide of L'Wren Scott, a famous fashion designer in New York who happened to be the girlfriend of Mick Jagger. The debate focused on the publication of a photo of Jagger distraught, having just been told of the news of the death of his lover. To publish or not was the question posed to one editor of a national newspaper. Press editors are leaders whether they acknowledge this or not, and their ethical choices lead public responses. So a choice to publish because Jagger lived his life in the public gaze once again brought into question what privacy is for famous people and, more importantly, the extent to which an editor will go to sell copies. Interestingly, the debate between the editor and photographer became heated, the latter seeing it as his job to be there and take the picture as an historical record.

The important point is that unless the editor has done the tough thinking about what he or she really stands for and would not be compromised over, how could he or she make such a delicate decision with the urgency needed? Moreover, with the unending pace of change and the demands on us to think instantly, largely as a result of technology, as leaders we have to be able to respond consistently. This is a key to being a responsible leader for the future. For example, Twitter, which we referenced earlier, allows instant communication to thousands, perhaps millions. This can be a powerful force for good and, as has been all too often the case, the source of embarrassment and even libel. At Nelson Mandela's funeral in December 2013, world leaders gathered to pay their respects to a remarkable man who embodied responsible leadership as fully as anyone has done. The joyful occasion got the better of the US president, the UK prime minister and the Danish prime minister, who when seated together decided to take a selfie (a photo of yourself on a smartphone). This innocuous event would have gone unnoticed but for Twitter and the modern social media. The photo was posted online, presumably by an observer, and became an instant global phenomenon. Sadly, people read into the scene motives that were probably not there, but it was clearly a somewhat insensitive thing to be doing at such an event – even if it was a celebration of a life well lived. Whether the US, UK and Danish leaders had thought about the context and how it would be received, we do not know. Nonetheless, had they thought about who might be seeing the photo or scene, and how it might impact their reputation, they might have thought differently. Modern leaders need to be wiser than simply being caught up in the moment.

Personal values do shape the decisions we make. Take, for example, the CEO of a small charity that I know of. He was presented with a dilemma. One of his small staff team had let herself down with some poor behaviour that was witnessed by others, albeit at a social event rather than in the normal course of work. Unfortunately, the event took place on the site of the charity. When asked what he wanted to do about the behaviour and ultimately what he wanted the action to be, he pondered for a while and then uttered a profound statement. 'If we are about giving young people a second chance, or a third chance in their often mixed-up lives, then we should do the same for one of our staff team as well.' He disciplined the individual but then encouraged her to take on more responsibility, to allow her to see herself in a different light – a bold and values-driven decision that led to a happy outcome and spoke volumes to colleagues and clients alike.

Throughout this book we will meet other men and women who embody responsible leadership. In my conversations with them and through my research, I have come to realize that they typically hold some clear beliefs that act as a source of energy for them. Values and beliefs are interwoven in their lives and find their way into, and are worked out through, their careers and how they lead. Be it a religious or spiritual faith, a belief in the inherent goodness of people or the integrity of nature, such beliefs embed themselves deeply in the soul of such people and inform their decisions.

A clear and established values and belief system also helps to smooth out irrational swings of behaviour (not always, of course) and leads to consistency. When people say of leaders 'you know where you stand with him or her', this is usually built on consistency of behaviour. As we will discover later, responsible leaders see the benefit in pausing to reflect and to recharge their energy. In these times they can draw on their belief systems as a source of insight to inform their day-to-day lives.

Moral compass

A third step to developing internal assuredness and attractiveness involves **rediscovering ethics and a moral compass.** We have already touched on this. The CEO in the previous example grappled with the ethics of care for his staff member but also care for the others in his team and his reputation. Ethics is a tough concept and yet something that most people would be all too quick to say that they fully embrace. Few leaders will openly admit to being unethical – quite the reverse. Consumers tend to be drawn to businesses that not only say that they 'do the right thing' but actually *do* the right thing. This point is very important, as almost every business I work with and many more besides actively state that one of their values or core purposes is 'to do the right thing', often for their stakeholders and communities and the wider world. This is laudable. Furthermore, it has now become the price of entry to the competition. The assumption now is that *all* organizations want to do the right thing. This means that the pressure is now on individuals and organizations to actually demonstrate this. And this is tough.

Earlier, we talked about Starbucks and the difficulties it encountered when it became clear that it was not paying what the press (and therefore public opinion) thought was a fair amount of corporation tax on its UK business. Despite operating within the parameters of the law, the company decided to make a payment by way of a gesture of goodwill in an attempt to redress the balance of opinion. For some this was seen as 'right', but for many others it was viewed as 'too little too late, and derisory'. Why?

In 2013, the Rana Plaza clothing factory building in Bangladesh collapsed, with the loss of over 1,300 lives and thousands more injured. Livelihoods were destroyed instantly. As the world watched the aftermath of the disaster, global retail brands scurried to find out if they were impacted. For those of us in the West, many of our garments are made in Bangladesh where labour costs are relatively cheap. The Clean Clothes Campaign has been set up to improve the conditions of workers in the clothing industry and is encouraging consumers to boycott large global retailers that have not contributed to a compensation fund for the victims. One UK retailer, Primark, which sourced many garments from the factory, did agree to pay the wages of all those people whose livelihoods were affected and this was applauded, but at the time of writing in 2014, almost one year on from the catastrophe, the wider fund has attracted support from only a handful of retailers. Why? Would it not be the right thing to do, perhaps?

What is clear is that this is a minefield where opinions differ and other forces begin to play on the minds of leaders of such organizations. These two examples are after-the-event moments. Perhaps what is more important as we look to responsible leaders is how to avoid such occurrences by proactive ethical practices. We will explore this aspect in more detail in subsequent chapters, but it is worthwhile highlighting one senior leader in a global business who has nailed his personal colours to the mast of ethical and moral standards. Paul Polman, CEO of Unilever, is a vocal advocate of doing things differently and championing ethical behaviours and practices. He has gone on record as supporting (and paying) higher wages in developing countries for workers creating Unilever brands locally, to build real trust and engagement. He has also openly admitted that he does not set much store by the short-term focus on share price and intends to hold firm to the long-term vision and perspective for Unilever around creating sustainable value and improving the quality of life for millions of people, often in developing countries, through the provision of basic, yet affordable, products.

Reflections

There are many thorough and helpful books and tools to help in the process of clarifying personal identity and internal assuredness. The following few prompts may act as a catalyst or a reminder for you:

- What are the important ingredients for you to be operating in your 'flow'?
- How could you describe you at your most effective and when you feel most fulfilled?
- What are the (few) key values that shape your behaviours and choices – eg what do you stand for – in your own words?
- Do you have a foundation of beliefs that you can draw on in your life inside and outside your work? If so, what are they and how do they manifest in your role? If not, how might you discover or reconnect with these?
- What does doing the right thing mean to you?
- When have you found or do you find it tough to 'do the right thing'?

Begin to craft your own statement of identity using these elements. Test it with others who know you well. Be open to refining it over time as you become clearer and consider working with a coach to help this process.

Adaptability and learning orientation

Once we have a strong centre that shapes our own unique internal assuredness and attractiveness, to be a responsible leader requires an orientation to learn, adapt and flex within this ambiguous world (see Figure 2.3).

FIGURE 2.3   The role of adaptability and learning orientation

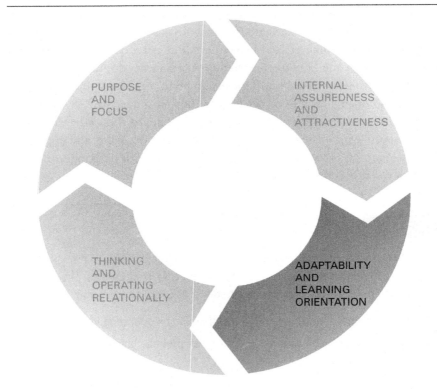

Comfortable with ambiguity and not knowing

With the rapid pace of the revolution that we discussed in the first chapter, it is a brave person who states for certain what will transpire in the next two years, let alone the next ten years. Volatility and uncertainty are prevailing forces operating seemingly unchecked. And paradoxically, businesses and markets crave stability to support investment decisions. What this suggests is that **leaders of tomorrow will need to be comfortable with 'not knowing', be able to model this confidently to their stakeholder groups and be at ease with fast-changing scenarios.**

What do we mean by 'not knowing'? It is about agility in decision-making and working with less than perfect or complete information. Typically the pattern might go something like this: Hierarchical structures require managers to produce detailed papers to present to committees higher up the organization for sign-off. Approval depends on the rational argument supported by data, evidence and reasoned argument. There is nothing wrong with that approach, of course, as it has operated for decades. However, given the new order, what if assumptions are made based on old thinking? For example, Morrisons, the fourth-largest supermarket in the UK, has for many years cherished its local family feel and has sought to represent this in its stores and in its adherence to a physical presence rather than join the internet presence which its competitors have been using successfully for a number of years. Late in 2013, the company realized that it needed to join the fray and took the decision to buy into Ocado as an online channel. Unfortunately for Morrisons, the company found itself falling well behind the pace and playing catch up. Slow decision-making processes and adherence to old paradigms may well have contributed to this scenario. Perhaps another factor adding to its tardiness was fear of the unknown that manifests as online presence and business – we do not know.

Not knowing fully how things will play out but acting on intuition and 'entrepreneurial instinct' is not new in business, and many successful business leaders have demonstrated significant agility over the recent past. Start-ups and technology-based businesses, often very small, proliferate now, largely because the revolution has enabled a climate in which being agile is rewarded. A recently established internet-based mail order business with a difference, called Graze, is promoting healthy-eating snacks and pushing them through letter boxes in attractive sustainable packaging: an example of a small company using new and old distribution channels and now challenging the way con-sumers snack. Earlier we identified BT CEO Gavin Patterson's courageous decision to go head to head with satellite broadcasters and compete for the lucrative sports TV market.

Sadly, this is not always replicated in the public sector, where entrenched positions and ways of working can inhibit responsiveness. Such reluctance to embrace the pace of the race has led to many public services in many developed economies now being taken over by third-sector and voluntary organizations. The case study later in this chapter highlights how one individual leader and his organization – Rev Steve Chalke and Oasis – have seized the opportunity to step into a space that is opening up to provide integrated education- and community-focused services. It is clear that Chalke relishes challenging the status quo and is prepared to offer alternative solutions to meet real needs.

Listening and learning

This leads us to a second aspect of adaptability – **curiosity and the willingness to learn and listen**. This may sound trite, but responsible leaders stand out from others through their hunger for feedback and learning. They are curious about their world and open to learning from many different sources. Again, this is not a new phenomenon, but in many respects it has become increasingly important both as the pace of change through new innovations demand it *and* as the forces of changing societal narratives pose tough questions for leaders. Many business leaders are now waking up to the fact that they should engage proactively with Generation Y and Millennials rather than relying on 'how we did things in my day'. Moreover, it is not just about engagement for engagement's sake. People see through 'tokenism'. No, what is now required is true dialogue and listening to understand before jumping to conclusions. Stephen R Covey (1992) awakened us all, somewhat prophetically it seems, to the concept of 'seek first to understand before being understood' in his seminal work *The Seven Habits of Highly Effective People*, first published in the late 1980s. Easy enough to say, but not to do. In our work with individuals and groups, we encounter situations where real listening and learning are needed for progress to be made. Covey's book is still an important reference work for responsible leaders. In it, the author tackles some simple truths and powerful behaviours that underpin personal effectiveness. In many ways, the work that we do with people, helping them develop their personal and responsible leadership for the future, builds on the foundations that he proposed. I will touch on some of these principles as we progress.

Recently, working in a large hospital to help develop better leadership, one of the primary observations was quite simply that expert clinicians and doctors were emotionally (and physically in some cases) disconnected from the management teams whose role it was to manage resources and budgets effectively. This led to a climate of suspicion, 'silo thinking' and working that not surprisingly manifested itself in disjointed practices overall. Importantly, in local teams and departments there was real excellence evidenced; it was just that it was not being shared or built upon. The pervading mindset was one of survival and protection rather than ambition and learning.

Unfortunately, it is a trait of human nature that when we become experts and accumulate knowledge we have a tendency to evaluate what we hear against our frames of reference and knowledge, thereby limiting our openness to hear differently or from surprising sources. We also believe that we can only learn from other experts or people who can speak in a language acceptable to us. We become judgemental and evaluative rather than inquisitive.

While working at PwC as Director of Leadership and Talent, I was fortunate to be involved in developing emerging leaders throughout the business. One important aspect of this programme was exposing emerging leaders to inspirational leadership from other sectors and environments. It is hard to rely on expert knowledge as an accountant when one is talking with a person who is leading drug rehabilitation work, for example. What becomes evident very early is that adopting a spirit of curiosity, enquiry and listening allows for understanding to develop. We will explore this as a method of developing responsible leaders in more detail in Part 2.

Open, confident yet humble

By way of a natural extension to the previous point, **responsible leaders are open, confident yet humble**. Moreover, they have personal resilience that comes from this. I do not propose to examine resilience in great detail in this book. There is much research going on at present about this, but what we do know is that individuals who demonstrate inner strength and personal resilience (necessary to deal with complexity in the modern VUCA world) are able to draw on their personal assuredness from a clear sense of their identity. This leads to an inner confidence. However, when this is not balanced with sober self-assessment or mature emotional intelligence, it becomes skewed and egocentric. It also closes people to other perspectives as these kinds of leader begin to believe their own propaganda and narrative and exclude others' perspectives. No, what appears to be a strong differentiator of companies that are able to sustain performance over time is what Jim Collins (in his seminal work *Good to Great*, 2001) referred to as 'tough humility' and a 'compelling modesty' in leaders. This work is an inspirational study of how some companies are able to move on from simply good performance and how leadership plays a key part in this process. This thinking has considerably informed our work on responsible leadership. Of the companies Collins researched, he found that the leaders were often referred to by their people as modest, quiet, humble, understated and self-effacing. They were also fiercely determined and not afraid to take tough decisions for the sake of the goals and the company. As we shall see later, responsible leaders create a climate and culture in which others excel and are inspired to perform. They are quick to give the glory to others rather than take it for themselves.

One person we shall meet more than once in this book is Richard Oldfield, a senior partner with global professional services firm PwC. Richard is one of the new breed of responsible leaders and was invited to lead a global team to pitch for the global audit of one of the world's largest companies. This account was currently held by a competitor and would be worth tens of millions of dollars to the victor. It was also one of the most complex and intricate accounts in the world of professional services – a significant prize to go for. When, after several months of focused effort, relationship-building and an onerous pitch process, the result of the tender process was announced, the company had decided to switch auditors and give the account to PwC. When I interviewed Richard Oldfield and asked him about this remarkable success – it was the biggest win in the sector for many years – he was modest about his contribution, preferring to say that it was all down to having a great team of people who brought some brilliant skills and motivation to the challenge. He also was quick to point out that a large aspect of the success was down to how the team built strong relationships throughout the client's network, creating connections that together meant they understood the business well. He was also under no illusions that he would need to rely on this great team to deliver great service across the globe to back up the success of the pitch, and that his role would be simply to keep the great people he had gathered together focused and enabled to deliver while sustaining relationships with key stakeholders in the company.

Being truly open is a mindset and orientation. It says to others that you are approachable and receptive – receptive to the possibility of new ideas, of fresh thinking, of criticism or coaching. As we shall continue to discover, the ability to work collaboratively with others sets apart responsible leaders and to do so effectively requires this open orientation; for example, knowing that I will get an appreciative reception when I bring a new way of working to the boss allows me to feel confident to take it in the first place.

Reflections

- What would being comfortable not knowing mean in your role and your organization?
- How can you encourage more agile responsiveness in your teams and throughout your organization?
- How are listening and a willingness to learn fostered in your organization?
- How much time and energy do you spend listening and learning?
- What images come to your mind when you think of openness and humility?
- What prevents openness and humility in your organization?

Thinking and operating relationally

The third component of our virtuous cycle (see Figure 2.4) involves a significant shift for many leaders. Brought up on completing the task and an achievement culture over the decades since the 1960s, many have forgotten, or perhaps ignored, the interdependent nature of our world. This requires re-engagement with the relational nature of our humanity.

FIGURE 2.4   The role of thinking and operating relationally

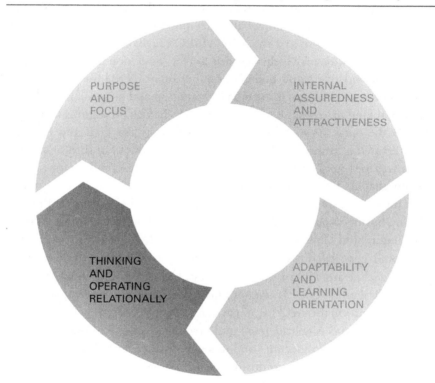

Moving from transactional to relational

If old hierarchies no longer enable the agility or response needed from leaders, and modern shapes for organizations become more flexible, leaders' perspectives of their leadership style need to adapt, and in one area specifically. Command and control, egocentric or autocratic approaches are being exposed as being short-termist, coercive and demotivating. Businesses' reputations have been damaged and in some cases destroyed by such approaches. Take for example The Royal Bank of Scotland (RBS), which at one point in the past ten years was in the top five banks in the world. It had grown rapidly from an essentially regional bank in the UK through aggressive acquisitions and a bold bancassurance structure (blending traditional banking, insurance and investment banking). In 2007 it put together a consortium of banks and won a dog-eat-dog fight for control of ABN AMRO against another interested bank, in this case Barclays, paying a staggering £49 billion for the deal. Many analysts considered this an excessively high price to pay. The acquisition backfired and failed to deliver any value added. The subsequent years have seen the complete collapse of the RBS share price, the virtual bankrupting of the organization and the ensuing bailout by the British taxpayer. The driving force behind the growth and the ABN AMRO takeover was the then CEO, Sir Fred Goodwin, a man widely regarded as a ferocious, domineering character who took no prisoners and bullied his subordinates. Fred the Shred (as he became known) revelled in his personal reputation and unassailable position as a virtual king of Scotland, where he built the bank's prestigious new head office in the outskirts of Edinburgh. Unfortunately for Fred and RBS, he simply created a culture in which no one dared speak out of turn or suggest alternatives for fear of being openly shouted down (quite literally, it transpired) and humiliated. The result was that a culture of fear prevailed in which group think took over and senior leaders began to believe their infallibility.

Many business schools will write case studies about the collapse of RBS. According to Jim Collins in his book *How the Mighty Fall* (2009), all the signs could have been spotted early. Collins identifies that the first three stages of decline are: Hubris Born of Success; Undisciplined Pursuit of More; Denial of Risk and Peril. Throughout his study, Collins draws out some key insights that inform this fresh paradigm of responsible leadership. For example, he pinpoints a 'success entitlement and arrogance' as one of the early signs of hubris (stage one of decline) and in stage two he shows how the 'unsustainable quest for growth, confusing big with great' and 'personal interests placed above organizational interests' contribute to a denial of reality that begins to take root. The decline can happen rapidly – within one or two years or even quicker – as was seen in the financial services industry in 2008 and, of course, in the now infamous case of Enron.

What is this telling us about responsible leadership? Often the study of the failures can inform us as effectively as studies of the successful, and this is beginning to help us define success differently – perhaps fundamentally.

As we are beginning to see, **to be truly responsible as a leader and organization, and to be effective in the next decades, is to regard oneself as** part of something bigger and thereby interdependent with other stakeholders. Sadly, Goodwin and other bankers (Dick Fuld of Lehmans, for example) regarded themselves and their organizations independently and as part of a zero-sum game in which competition and winning at all costs was the goal. Growth and size, profitability (in some cases illusory) and personal status became the only measures of success.

Moving from competition to co-creation

The future paradigm suggests that success will be more relational than transactional. S G Warburg, one of the founders of modern-day investment banking, was famous for his principles and how he put people and relationships at the centre of his work. 'For me the greatest interest and enjoyment were human relations,' he said about what got him into banking. 'Human matters,' he wrote in 1957, 'are much more important than business affairs.' This was a principle to which he remained true all his life. Sadly, modern-day bankers have lost sight of clients as people, driven as they are to deliver short-term results and enact the transaction.

Competition is not bad. It fosters commitment and can provide genuine focus for energy. I for one believe that competition can help some people (not all, I must stress) tap into their innate drives, which in turn allows them to be at their best and most creative. We see this often in great individual sportsmen and women who pull out a remarkable shot or play from seemingly nowhere. However, the world is shifting and expectations of society and customers are now focusing on longer-term factors, including contributions to communities, environmental sustainability and learning. Stakeholders are looking for evidence of integrity, trustworthiness, generous gestures – values-based behaviour. And as we have seen, in times when substitution of goods and services is easy, business leaders will do well to remind themselves of this.

Furthermore, future opportunities are more likely to be grabbed by businesses and individuals who model collaboration. A coaching client of mine is a senior professional adviser and part of our coaching has included how this individual transitions from one important client relationship on to a bigger role, which is good for his career. He wrestled with how to tell his client about the switch of its account to another colleague, fearing that he would be seen as letting it down somehow. We explored the nature of his thinking, which for him is founded on his strong sense of personal values and on loyalty in particular. It also became clear that he had been working *with* his client over the last few years to help it tackle some very difficult issues in the business, and in particular around some mistakes that it had made in the past, the results of which were now coming home to haunt it. My client's generous approach to offer and co-create solutions *with* his client had created an atmosphere of genuine trust and respect. He was not there to judge on right or wrong, but to help it move forward and rebuild. He recounted to me how the CEO of his client had wept with him over the dilemmas that he was facing and the questions about how he could re-establish his business's reputation and brand – true relational leadership in operation.

Co-creation is a mindset that requires a fundamental orientation of generosity in the hope of mutual growth, not the expectation of such. Creating anything – art, literature, inventions, new businesses – involves personal risk and entertaining the prospect of disappointment. With it, though, comes the prospect of something remarkable and synergistic.

The realm of politics is a dangerous place to visit, but I will draw on one example of how co-creation has changed the landscape of a population. For over 40 years, from the 1960s, Northern Ireland was the scene of religious tensions that have spilt over into sectarian violence of the worst kind. As the decades unfolded, positions became even more entrenched and atrocities more shocking. I grew up on the mainland of the UK watching this from afar, until the Troubles spread to the mainland with terrorist bombs in other British cities. Without going into the details of the transformation, since the turn of the century there has been a truly remarkable change, based in part on the change in relationship between two political giants in Northern Ireland – Ian Paisley (Unionist) and Martin McGuinness (IRA) – who for years held an animosity that was clear for all to see. And yet, presumably, their belief in trying to create a future that was more sustainable for their stakeholders was a more powerful force than division based on history. Moreover, their personal desire to leave a different legacy, coupled with advancing age and perhaps acquired wisdom, led them to work together and, so it would seem, become great friends who laughed together in public – co-creators of a future that embraces tensions yet finds a way through. Whether it holds and how long it lasts is uncertain, but as an act of responsible leadership it is a compelling story.

Moving from self to other

These examples highlight an aspect of the new paradigm that is beginning to set responsible leaders apart, namely their view of themselves in relation to others. As human beings we will always have a self-protection drive, and yet, increasingly perhaps, those whose perspective of success relies on others' success are becoming a stronger force than perhaps many realize. Throughout history, wise leaders have realized that it is a leverage model that is the real measure of success for a leader – namely the extent to which more can be achieved through enabling and empowering others rather than through one's own efforts.

In these revolutionary times, many of the world's spiritual leaders, such as the Dalai Lama, Pope Francis and Archbishop Justin Welby, are being listened to with greater attention as they not only speak about, but model, selfless behaviours. Younger generations are asking questions of themselves and society that are calling for meaning. Older generations are asking tough questions about legacy. Academics are challenging their own assumptions and theories. The French economist Thomas Piketty in his recent book *Capital in the Twenty-first Century* (2014) raises some uncomfortable questions about the extent to which markets can regulate distribution of wealth and asks if we can ever control the magnetic pull of wealth to an increasingly small number of people around the globe.

A positive voice and emerging movement is that of 'Otherish' as championed by Professor Adam Grant in his recent work *Give and Take* (2013). Grant highlights how successful givers balance a high concern for self-interest with a high concern for others' interests by recognizing that being generous in sharing information, power and wealth through relationships and networks reaps reputational and tangible rewards. He quotes Bill Gates at the World Economic Forum, who argued that 'there are two great forces of human nature: self-interest and caring for others' and went on to propose a hybrid of **motivational drives that are not mutually exclusive, namely to be genuinely interested in care and benefit of others while being focused on achieving what each of us wants as an individual.** Grant calls this 'Otherish', which is a profound principle of responsible leadership.

In business and organizations this can manifest in many ways, but one that is common in my experience is the degree to which leaders hold on to or release talented individuals. In my work around talent management I come across many inspiring leaders who have worked out that by gaining a reputation for developing people through handing over power and responsibility, they gain a reputation for being great to work with and great leaders. In so doing, they then attract better talent who want to work for such a leader. And what follows is typically increased performance from the whole team or business. The important point to note here is that there is an upfront cost and investment of time and energy that is essentially 'Otherish' on the part of the responsible leader, not to mention a considerable degree of personal risk. One exemplar of this is Paul Polman, Global CEO of Unilever, the giant consumer goods multinational. Unilever is doing some things that are setting it apart from other multinationals in the area of responsible leadership and much of it is driven by Polman, the visionary Dutchman at the helm. In a recent interview with the *Guardian* in the UK, he was quoted as saying: 'Often people ask me what my job is and I say honestly it is make others successful, and the more you do that the more you will see that you create prosperity.'

Regrettably, I also come across leaders whose fear of loss of power or control manifests itself in damaging protectionist behaviours, often to maintain current levels of performance rather than aspire to step change. Perversely, this is most evident in organizations that compete for talent through offering increasingly extravagant remuneration packages, attracting as they do self-focused individuals (some would say mercenaries) to protect revenue streams, for example, only to find that such individuals are easily tempted by a better offer in due course, and who do not pass on their expertise or insights. It is not a surprise that the talent pool in the world of financial services is one that simply moves from one organization to another in a spiral of increasing remuneration, which in turn drives up costs and bonuses that in turn attract louder complaint and disgust from society at large. S G Warburg would be turning in his grave at the shame.

Reflections

- Whom do you admire as a role model in this area?

- How is co-creation demonstrated in and through your organization?

- How do you personally model a balanced relational and task approach to leading?

- Whom can you work with in your organization to create a more relational culture?

- What hinders you and your organization from being more 'otherish'?

Purpose and focus

Our final point in this chapter is a profoundly simple one (see Figure 2.5): **responsible leaders have a guiding purpose that enables them to focus their**

FIGURE 2.5 The role of purpose and focus

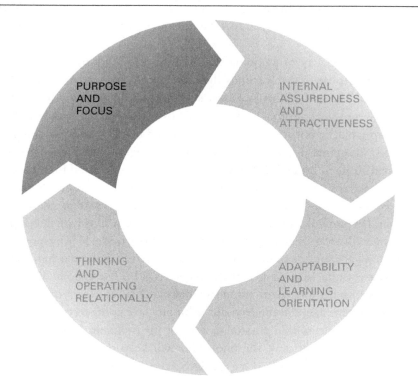

energy and activity. This sense of purpose is more than making money and delivering value simply to shareholders. As a driving force, this has been found to be blinkered. Paul Polman of Unilever is committed to a long-term approach to his business and has been outspoken about the short-termism he sees in the need to deliver quarterly statements to the financial markets. For him, his business is about something deeper and more lasting, providing as it does fundamental products that improve life for millions around the world and increasingly in emerging markets and developing countries where access to hygiene products has been historically poor.

In the face of the storm of revolution, as we have seen, it is easy to be reactive and jump on the latest bandwagon or fad. Nowhere is this truer than in the C-suites of the corporate world, especially when it comes to ticking the corporate social responsibility (CSR) boxes to say that 'our business is here for the good of the community and environment'. And this may indeed be the case, but it will only be true when leaders make bold and courageous decisions to stop certain behaviours and practices and encourage more radical choices. For example, deciding to pay above-average wages in developing territories or to stop doing business with sectors such as gambling or short-term loan companies that seek to take advantage of the disadvantaged of society.

However, one way of avoiding the constant knee-jerking is to **have an overriding purpose** that transcends these pressures. The late Anita Roddick – founder of The Body Shop – was one such person. Bursting on the scene in 1976 with a radical approach to retailing cosmetics (asking people to take back empty plastic bottles to be refilled), she and her husband Gordon built The Body Shop into a global phenomenon such that the giant business that is L'Oréal chose to bring it under its umbrella for what it stood for and what it could teach the bigger business. And yet Roddick herself was not motivated at all by money or growth of the business. Her drive was to change the world and in particular the way established economies traded with developing economies. She was in many ways the mother of fair trade. Her purpose was so much bigger for her than a retail business. That was the mechanism for her to outwork her vision and calling. In her book *Body and Soul* (1992) she concludes with her long-term visionary thinking: 'I believe that young people of my daughter's age, the children of the hippies, are going to come forward with a moral code, with a passion, a zest for the moment, and prove to be the true planetary citizens, the ones who will keep this planet alive. My generation has certainly not done much to keep it going.'

The extent to which she saw the vision realized by the time she died in 2007 (sadly aged only 65) I believe is encapsulated in much of the revolution that we talked about earlier in this book. Emerging generations and society at large are now asking profoundly uncomfortable questions about sustainability and stewardship, especially of business leaders and politicians. I am sure she would be content with this and yet still driving us on as we seek to develop more responsible leadership practices.

For Roddick, this purpose consumed her energy and passion. She toured the world developing sustainable self-financing trading businesses and was single-minded in her determination. I once met her and heard her speak, in a somewhat disorganized way, to a gathering of business leaders. What was without question, though, was her passion and forthrightness in her conviction. It was compelling and inspiring, driving me to further explore responsible leadership.

Clearly, not everyone can have such a big vision. Let me introduce you to Rob, who runs a small charity that provides learning opportunities for young people in a beautiful and stimulating outdoor setting on the edge of London. Young people from inner London arrive to be greeted by a dog and the smell and sounds of an organic farm. Their normal worlds are a million miles from this. Often they have been discarded by mainstream education and branded as misfits with severe behavioural or learning difficulties. To Rob and his team, they are human beings who have probably been misunderstood or worse, abused or living in impossibly difficult family circumstances. Rob sees his purpose and that of his team as being to treat them with dignity and respect, to encourage them, to love them, to challenge them if need be and, above all, to believe in them. His strapline is 'Inspired to inspire', which provides a clear mantra for him and his team and his clients. His Lambourne End Centre for Outdoor Learning sets out to find ways to inspire young people and their teachers or carers to achieve and believe, and when they are uplifted they in turn inspire the people they come into contact with and the team back at the outdoor learning centre. He has many stories of schools and communities reporting dramatic changes in behaviour. Moreover, he has many stories of young people whose lives have been turned around and they have gone on to further education or employment, when most people in their system said it was unlikely.

Leaders with a strong driving purpose – that answers the *'why am I doing this?'* question – need commensurate levels of **focus to ensure that their dreams and visions do not remain out of reach**. In my work I encounter this in many forms. It can be a single-minded stubbornness or unwavering perseverance. It can be courageous decision-making that is prepared to cut losses or step out into the unknown. Always it is where the leader focuses his or her attention. The question being answered is *'What do I need to do and what is important for me/us?'* If you will, *'Where do I need to focus my attention and my energy and therefore what are distractions to be avoided?'*

By way of example, a coaching client of mine who I will call Gareth was an exemplar at building and sustaining relationships with his clients. As we talked about his leadership of his business team he became increasingly frustrated that many of the younger people coming through in his business were fearful of building relationships and unskilled in doing so. The result was that business opportunities were potentially being missed, but more important for Gareth was that people didn't seem to 'get the importance of this in their business'. Gareth was so focused on his clients that he would spend much of his waking life speaking with them, meeting them, getting to know them, such that he became their trusted adviser and they respected him. On one occasion during a coaching session, when one of his clients walked past the window, Gareth caught sight of him and quickly asked if I minded if he got up and said hello. As a responsible leader, Gareth's challenge is now to find ways to communicate that passion to his colleagues and those whom he is mentoring. Supporting, training, coaching and encouraging them will need to be part of his focus, and he knows this. Significantly, this is totally aligned to *his* purpose and focus – to help his clients be better at what they do.

Reflections

- Can you articulate your driving purpose and answer the 'why am I doing this' question clearly?

- How do you communicate this to those you work with?

- To what extent are you disciplined in aligning your activities and priorities with this purpose?

- What hinders you doing this?

CASE STUDY   Rev Steve Chalke MBE and Oasis

As we search for stories of responsible leaders and leadership, it is helpful for us to remain open-minded and cast our net more widely than the obvious places. There is much now to learn from places other than the corporate world. One such place is the so-called third sector and the burgeoning social enterprise arena. There are numerous examples of a next generation of responsible leaders emerging in the UK and around the world, many of whom have started from small beginnings and now, by virtue of the interconnected world, find themselves more in the public's gaze. In south London, one charity and social enterprise is modelling responsible leadership through its work in the community. In 2013 I met its founder and explored with him the questions facing leaders in the 21st century and how his organization is modelling responsible leadership.

Background to the story

The story of Oasis involves a remarkable man, Steve Chalke, his vision, and how he has been able to inspire thousands of people around the world to work with him to realize it. Born in south London in the 1950s, Chalke's future was shaped from the outset by his genealogy. Coming from a mixed-race family – his father was born in southern India and his mother in the UK – he found himself different from others. In the 1950s, mixed-race marriages were rare and the young Chalke grew up in a degree of poverty. He does not think his childhood was bad by any means, but it was a struggle in the years that shaped the multiracial and multinational culture that we now take for granted. In such an environment of a struggle to be confident in one's identity, Chalke recognizes that he was equipped with a personal resilience, a real sense of justice and an understanding of inclusion and diversity. It's this that shapes his personal vision and, importantly, how this has been worked out through Oasis.

The vision

When you meet Chalke or hear him communicate in the media, you are instantly struck by a huge smile and a humble confidence. You also soon appreciate that he is a consummate storyteller who is not afraid to challenge assumptions and paradigms. He narrates richly, powerfully and with a smidgeon of humour the moment when, aged 14 and having realized that the girl of his dreams was out of his reach, he resolved to build a school and hostel and a hospital to model how communities should be. He saw that these were not working well in his local community and elsewhere. Whether this was an overreaction or a calling, it is clear that this man is a man on a mission. And the mission is to transform communities in the UK and beyond these shores.

Chalke's vision is shaped profoundly by his faith and by his foundational belief in a society that is open, welcoming, inviting and inclusive. He trained as a Baptist minister and currently leads Oasis Church Waterloo, which is based at The Oasis Centre. However, what marks out Chalke as a modern and responsible leader is his systemic perspective. At an early age his natural gifts of perception and drive combined to enable him to see that communities are critical to well-being and society's fabric, and then to urge him forward to push against boundaries in the *established* system to fight injustice and exclusion. His natural strength to galvanize and bring people together, often from differing camps, to tackle thorny issues has enabled him to garner support from right across the political and business spectrum. It has also found him confronting deeply held views, not least within the wider Christian arena that he inhabits.

Oasis – the journey

Chalke embarked on his vision to combat injustice and build communities in 1985 and, typical of his longer-term view, his first action was to start a personal development training programme for young volunteers working in churches across the UK. After three years, he had close to a hundred advocates for the vision.

In 1989, Chalke launched Christmas Cracker, an appeal to raise funds for projects among the poorest groups of people in the world, tapping into the younger generation's questioning and a post-Live Aid awareness of issues in the developing world. This campaign has raised millions over the years and laid the foundations for Oasis's extraordinary impact. A key thread running through Oasis's work is its apparent ability to consistently punch above its weight by tapping into the zeitgeist and being bold in its ambition – for the greater good.

There followed projects started in India and the rest of the subcontinent, working to train women in clothes-making and design skills, supporting people living with HIV and AIDS; in Central and Southern Africa, focusing on education; in São Paulo, working with the disadvantaged.

Early in the new millennium, Chalke's vision to help people living difficult lives in difficult situations began to focus on human trafficking; this took him into North America and was the start of his work with human trafficking for which he is now an appointed Special Advisor on Community Action to the United Nations Global Initiative to Fight Human Trafficking (UN.GIFT). His *Stop The Traffik* book (2009) was co-authored with Tony Blair's wife Cherie and has led to a global following of tens of thousands, debate in parliaments the world over, and, importantly, real action taken by renowned corporates in the global chocolate market (for example, Nestlé and Cadbury) in response to a Fairtrade initiative to eradicate trafficking in the chocolate industry.

In 2003 Oasis opened its hub in Waterloo, south London, where it now runs two schools, several football teams, a community café, numerous education classes, a recording studio, youth work, mentoring schemes, debt advice, a food bank and other projects across the local area.

This model has now begun to be rolled out across the UK as Oasis has proved itself hugely attractive as a provider of quality schooling, taking advantage of the changes in the educational landscape and specifically the academy initiative introduced in the mid-2000s. The charity now runs over 40 schools and academies around the UK, making it a driving force in the new shape of education in the UK (and overseas – there are schools opening in Africa under the Oasis umbrella).

Another example of how the charity operates systemically and relationally is the People's Parliament. Through a series of conversations Oasis brings together politicians, members of the civic society and community, business leaders and social entrepreneurs to debate important issues impacting the nation and its communities. Held in Waterloo and contrary to what you might imagine about pseudo-left-wing protest debates, these events have attracted government ministers to discuss with the man on the Clapham omnibus thorny issues such as leadership trust, bankers' bonuses and immigration, to name just a few.

A look at the Oasis website is an inspiring glimpse into a different future in which the possible is not just envisioned but made to happen. A visit to their hub in Waterloo reveals an organization with strong values modelled by the people who work there. The building is not pretentious in any way (indeed Chalke himself has a virtually subterranean office devoid of the trappings associated with similar high-profile figures), being commensurate with the local surroundings of inner London.

Learning and insights

Chalke's view on leadership is that it is a journey, both a personal and an organizational one. He believes that it is a process of internal discovery and refinement alongside a process of external outworking. He himself recognizes that his vision is being refined as it is outworked and that as a key leadership figure, his role is to keep telling the story and finding ways of keeping the vision and values alive. He has little time for corporates that simply adorn their office spaces with values words or vision statements, expecting that this will lead miraculously to a culture in which they are lived out in all that goes on.

He is intentional in shaping the culture across all the different parts of Oasis, and has established a Central Ethos Team. He asserts that just as a mainstream corporate would not dream of operating without a finance function, his charity has to live and breathe the ethos that holds it together and that a team drawn from across the business can play a proactive role in finding ways for the culture to be reinforced, continually.

His view is that paying attention to the roots of the business is fundamental to its fruit and growth. He suggests that too many organizations and businesses lose sight of what is important because they spend too much time focusing 'on the foliage', which, he advocates, includes short-term performance goals rather than longer-term impact. What people *believe* about themselves and the organization shapes the collective character and how they as individuals behave and make decisions. In Oasis, everyone knows this.

For Chalke, he is determined that his HR department is different from the 'how best to get rid of people'-driven corporate HR functions populated by unhappy processors. He wants an HR team that is all about winning people's hearts and minds, facilitating them to deliver the vision as an inspired individual. Indeed, Oasis has an internal course simply called 'Life', the primary focus of which is to help their people become the best version of themselves they can be.

The future

At Oasis, their ethos is shaped around key principles of inclusion, equality, relationship, hope and perseverance. As we explore the future for Chalke and

Oasis, he is quick to stress that it starts from a relationship orientation and that for communities to flourish where they have been neglected in the recent past, people need to feel that they can trust others (and leaders) and that they are understood as individuals.

Oasis champions connectedness, something that stems directly from Chalke's original vision of communities being places of genuine support and growth. The parallels with the Quaker leaders of the 18th and 19th centuries are not lost on Chalke either. For them, their business visions were implemented through creating new models of worker and community involvement, often by developing an integrated system of housing, care, employment, social activity, education and health. Many of these lasted for decades and shaped a new way of thinking, and while not all Quakers followed this model, their principles of trust and honesty in business and respect for their workers' contributions and well-being are well documented. In her book, *Chocolate Wars*, Deborah Cadbury (2010) provides a rich history of the evolution of this thinking against the backdrop of the emerging chocolate industry, bringing to life some of the great characters of that era in the UK, Europe and the United States.

Interestingly, modern charities and some businesses, through CSR Foundations, are now repeating these models overseas in developing economies such as Africa and India. Oasis is one such enterprise and is unashamed in its drive to model a different way of community relevant for the 21st century, both in developing economies and importantly in the UK itself.

Reflecting on the nature of leaders and leadership that will be effective in the future, Chalke is clear in his views that the future of leadership is going to be about character and not just skill. He uses his preacher's gift of storytelling to illustrate his focus on the need for humility and authenticity in effective leaders. Leaders who can model servanthood, who can walk with people and listen to people, will, in his view, connect more easily and build trust more naturally.

Finally, and somewhat typical of the agent provocateur that is Steve Chalke, he raises the question of social media and the challenge that leadership needs to adapt quickly to embrace the complex issues it presents. He mentions that many business leaders and politicians have been very quick to jump on the social media bandwagon, only to have been found out as shallow. Globalization and the internet have given access to all the content and information we need, in his view, but what people are missing and are craving is local meaning – someone they know whom they can rely on and trust. As he puts it, the tension between knowing what to say to the wider world and how to translate meaning for local communities has never been more real.

What can we learn from this about responsible leadership?

- The responsible leader sees things as interconnected and interdependent.

- The responsible leader is both future focused and grounded firmly in the present, the here and now, and the practical on-the-ground impact of actions.

- Responsible leadership is about connecting at a deeper level with stakeholders – at the soul, story and heritage level that provides meaning for staff teams, communities and customers.

- The narrative is aligned with the vision across the wider organizational system through a culture that the leader role models wholeheartedly and authentically, often at considerable personal risk.

- Responsible leaders know who they are, what they stand for, and are not afraid to step forward, even at personal risk. They are passionate and can inspire others through their personal energy, commitment and sense of purpose.

Summary

In the next chapter we will explore how these paradigms are outworked within a wider system – one in which we all operate to some degree or another. In this chapter we have sought to highlight some important paradigms that we see evident and operating in responsible leaders. Typically:

- They have internal assuredness and attractiveness:
  - They lead from an authentic core that resonates with others.
  - They stand for something and are values led.
  - They operate from a strong moral compass.
- They are adaptable and oriented to learn:
  - They are comfortable not knowing and are at ease with fast-changing scenarios.

- They listen and learn well.
- They are open, confident, yet humble.
- They think and operate relationally:
  - They move from transactional to relational.
  - They move from competition to co-creation.
  - They move from self to other.
- They inspire others with their purpose and focus:
  - They have a clear answer to the question 'why am I doing this?'
  - They think through carefully the answers to the questions 'where do I need to focus my energy?' and 'what is important to me?'

Reflections

- As you read through these points, which resonate loudly for you and why? Do you agree with them?

- As you think about your own situation and relationships, who comes to mind for you as embodying these well and why? Perhaps people come to mind who are in leadership positions in your 'world' but who do not embody these at all well.

- To what extent are these points true of you and your organization?

- What would people be saying about you and how you embody these paradigms?

What it means to be a responsible leader in practice

03

*We were not meant to stand alone. We need to belong –
to something or someone. Only where there is a mutual
commitment will you find people prepared to deny
themselves for the good of others.*

(CHARLES HANDY, *THE EMPTY RAINCOAT*)

Having explored a simple model of factors that differentiate responsible leaders for the future, we need to begin to identify what this means in practice. For me, responsible leadership is both actions and an orientation. It is the choices that an individual and an organization take based on a mindset that embraces complexity and finds ways to simplify it in order to make progress. During this chapter we will:

- share and explore a holistic picture in three levels of the system in which responsible leaders can make a difference;
- identify how the responsible leader can use a relational mindset based on an authentic core to thrive in the organizational system;
- show how organizations and leaders need to be mindful of the macro-perspectives of planet, economy and community;
- pose some initial challenges for you and your organization as you continue to reflect on your response.

CASE STUDY   HSBC Mexico

As we invited each of the participants to work on a narrative that helped bring their strategy alive, neither my co-facilitator nor I expected the story told to the group by Alfonso. We had been working with a group of senior leaders at the Mexico head office of HSBC and the topic of our workshop was around helping them develop the skills needed to be heads of functions and responsible leaders. One such skill is the ability to narrate a strategy in ways that inspire the people called upon to outwork the strategy. This has been true of responsible leaders for generations and our client was realizing that this was needed now more than ever before.

Alfonso's story went broadly like this. 'Picture the scene,' he said. 'You have in front of you a school full of small children in a poor provincial town in rural Mexico. Their faces are despondent and the head teacher explains that it is largely because they do not have any uniforms for school that they were promised by the local authority. The local authority had sourced the uniforms from a local manufacturer and had secured a good price for the bulk order for uniforms for all the schools in the district. Unfortunately, the manufacturer had been working on a price for their raw materials that suddenly spiked as the global price of cotton leapt following commodity speculations. The regional manufacturer was left high and dry and not able to fulfil the orders.'

Alfonso continued. 'Then imagine,' he said, 'that you, a senior leader of our bank here in Mexico, are talking with the regional governor. Because we have finance factoring services, we said to the governor that we would work with him and the local suppliers to provide finance that would smooth out the spike and allow the manufacturer to fulfil the order. A deal is done and the cotton secured. The machines spring back into life and the uniforms begin to roll off the production line. Now imagine you are standing in the same school a month later and all the children are wearing smart new uniforms. Their mood is now completely different and, more to the point, they can trust their head teacher to keep his word.' Alfonso's *coup de grâce* was: 'And *we* did that. We made that happen. We put smiles back on the faces of the children and reinforced trust in their community. That is our strategy at work.'

The group spontaneously applauded Alfonso for he had in a masterstroke delivered an inspiring narrative that brought people fully into his thinking and brought the strategy alive. Moreover, he had, unconsciously he admitted, described the responsible leadership model in action. It was a powerful moment that I suspect Alfonso's fellow senior leaders in the bank will never forget.

Learning and insight

Fundamental to being a responsible leader in action is thinking holistically and systemically. Alfonso realized that he was an agent in a bigger system and that he had the power to impact that system – positively. His organization had given him the tools to do this through the provision of their services and product offering, and the organizational strength of brand made it more likely that the regional politicians and the producers of the cotton would work to find a way forward.

This story brings to life a model that I and a number of my colleagues have been developing over the past few years. This part of the book deals with this model in more depth. The previous case study about Rev Steve Chalke and Oasis also demonstrates this model in practice.

Figure 3.1 shows the full model and the first thing that I want to highlight is that it is a holistic representation of a system. It is not a linear left to right (or right to left, for that matter) process. There is no 'do this followed by that'. In many respects, this model is more of a representation of what is apparent. When I work with groups exploring their particular system, we encourage them to stand and engage fully with the system as if it were a moving three-dimensional sculpture (I shall return to this in Part 2). I have found that it is important for people not to only get it intellectually but to feel it and to process it emotionally and spiritually.

When leaders acknowledge that they are playing a part within a wider system and that their agency can – indeed will inevitably – impact this system, they become powerful. Such realization can, of course, lead to a negative or a positive engagement. Irresponsible leaders, like some of those that we have met already, set out to manipulate the system for *their* own ends, their company's goals at the expense of the other members of the system. They tend to have a narrow view of their relationships, seeing them as predominantly transactional in nature. Typically, their belief in a wider system is short term and predicated on a utilization mindset, namely, how can I or we use this to get what we want?

On the other hand, responsible leaders begin to realize that their agency can be intentional. They see that it is possible for the wider whole to benefit from the interactions and the interdependencies. They have a deep-seated belief in a generative mindset based on what is possible, while being acutely aware of the inherent tensions within the system. **Responsible leaders tend to focus on embracing the uncertainties and paradoxes rather than trying to fix them.**

FIGURE 3.1   Responsible leadership: a holistic model

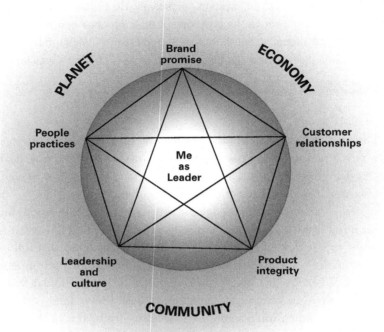

At the core

In the centre of the system is the individual – me and you as a leader. We cannot leave it at that, though. Critical to the effectiveness of a responsible holistic system and model is the orientation of the core. When I and my colleagues work with groups and individuals, we call this *the authentic self as core.*

Regrettably, many of our coaching clients find themselves in roles and functions that they did not sign up to and that feel alien to them or incongruent with who they are, sometimes the result of things changing around them, sometimes because they have made a poor career choice, sometimes because they have lost sight of who they are. Whatever the reason, they struggle to find their authentic self. It is not unusual for it to be the case that the more senior a person, the more of a pretence is needed to fit in with an organizational culture or expectations of colleagues or wider stakeholders, for example the markets, the public, politicians and so on. Equally, young and ambitious career-minded individuals can sometimes be prone to dilute their true selves and values, adopting what they believe to be needed.

Responsible leaders are first and foremost authentic. They know who they are and do not pretend to try to be someone else. Ian Powell, Chairman of PwC UK, is a quietly spoken man from the West Midlands who rose through the firm to become its leader in 2008. A West Bromwich Albion football supporter who went to Wolverhampton University, Powell did not fit many people's idea of the City operator at the time. And yet, drawing on his strong personal values, acquired from his strong family and community upbringing, he is a man who is first and foremost approachable and who creates a climate in which people can be themselves. At a lecture he gave to a business school, when asked about his leadership, he replied that being authentic was at the core because it just took too much effort to pretend to be someone you are not all the time. It is much more efficient and engaging to be yourself and then others can decide whether they want to work with you or not.

In our work, we encourage people to clarify their personal authentic core based on:

- an accurate understanding of their own sense of identity (which we have touched on already) in terms of strengths, uniqueness, personality and values;
- a sense of their personal life vision and legacy, their purpose if you will – what it is that, over time, they feel they want to achieve and/or leave behind;
- a realization of their talent and capability, both natural and learnt, that they can draw upon in their life and work.

It is worth reminding ourselves of these in a little more depth.

Reflections

- Being honest with yourself, how much effort have you spent on exploring your own personal 'centre', and how effective has that been?
- To what extent do you enable people in your team or organization to do this for themselves?

Core identity

Over the years, we have learnt that identity needs to precede function. When a person (or a team or an organization) has a clear sense of who they are, decisions about careers or opportunities or indeed dilemmas become easier and more straightforward. Typically, we will spend time with someone exploring their unique strengths, as we mentioned previously – helping them find out when they are in the flow. We enable people to identify their values over which they won't compromise and how these shape their behaviour. Often this is woven with their personality (using various well-known diagnostic tools) to help explain why they typically behave in a particular way or have a specific leadership style. We work to help them build a balanced self-awareness and appreciation. I do not intend to go into a lot more detail about this, primarily because it requires deep investigation that would be better done at another time. I can recommend Strengths Finder as a valuable introduction based on the book *Now, Discover Your Strengths* (Buckingham and Clifton, 2004) – a helpful and well-used tool that when supported by coaching can facilitate greater self-understanding.

Reflections

- Can you, honestly, say that you know clearly what your strengths are, and can you summarize them succinctly?
- To what extent would others agree with your assessment?

Life vision, legacy and purpose

In the previous chapter we identified that purpose is critical to responsible leadership thinking. Here we position this as an important aspect of an authentic core. Leaders like Anita Roddick and Richard Branson seem to have a remarkable sense that they have a larger vision. The former we have examined already. The latter, apart from being head of a global brand that confronts established operating models, is also an important player on the global stage of conflict mediation, helping coordinate The Elders (a group of former world leaders that works behind the scenes to intervene in politically and emotionally charged disputes around the world). They were instrumental in bringing a peaceful resolution to the post-election crisis in Kenya in 2008, a fact not widely reported. This allows him to operate from a strong sense of justice, of right and wrong. Bill Gates, the founder of Microsoft who has built up an astonishing fortune, has gone on record as saying that he intends to give away much of it in the cause of tackling global diseases and health issues on a gigantic scale through his Foundation, which he runs with his wife Melinda. Now whether he set out to do that when he devised the Microsoft operating system is unlikely. At that time, his vision was more likely to push the boundaries of the new technology and learning, and he had an opportunity through timing and great skill that allowed him to dominate this sector. However, his vision to have impact has taken a different course subsequently, still pushing the boundaries I should point out, but in this case the boundaries of our thinking and practice around tackling global diseases such as malaria among the poorest communities on the planet.

Most of us cannot hope to have such fame and fortune around which to build our legacy, and yet when we meet people who have a sense of making an impact or difference even in a small way through a local business or community, it is naturally attractive. Earlier we met Rob, the CEO of the small charity working with young people. His vision and legacy are local and he can name many of the players involved in its outworking.

Reflections

- As you reflect on your own centre, what would you like to be your personal legacy in your current role, and if you can think that far ahead, in your wider life?

- What will help you achieve this legacy and what will stop you?

Talent and capability

Recently I found myself working with a group of professional services partners, helping them work out their strategic priorities for the next few years. This is a critically important leadership task and during the workshop we explored their collective identity and how they wanted to be known by their stakeholders across their wider system. Towards the end of the session, the group's leader announced that he had been approached to consider a new role in the wider organization and was very vexed about how he should proceed. A number of his colleagues voiced their feelings: a mixture of being pleased for him, of not being surprised that he was being considered, but also of uncertainty about how his change of focus might impact their business in what were tricky times for them. Later, when speaking with this individual, we discussed the reactions and his choices. What was (and still is) apparent was the high regard in which this authentic man was held by his peers and how his leadership approach had produced results over the past few years. I drew his attention to his innate talent for empathy and emotional intelligence, and how his openness to learning has led him to deepen this. He is a man who is deeply interested in others and how to optimize their talents, and this is demonstrated through his approachability, his genuine care for the people in his business, his gentle manner balanced with resolve and his sense of being on a journey of discovery himself. Over time, he has learnt how to communicate more succinctly and to use his passion skilfully. He has enhanced his natural talent for relationships to become naturally himself and highly regarded because of this.

People and leaders who spend time investigating their innate talents, like my client, and honing these over time while accepting their shortcomings are people whose authentic core becomes both magnetic and enabling. Conversely, a reluctance to do so results in what I refer to as the doughnut approach, in which the individual is trying to navigate the complexities of the system from an empty core at worst or flaky foundations that lead to a predominantly reactive orientation. And in times of uncertainty, as we have seen already and will expand upon further, striking the balance between proactivity and reaction fosters agility.

Reflections

- To what extent can you articulate your individual authentic core in ways that would be inspiring for others to follow?

- Which aspects require further clarification or honing for you, and how might you do that?

- Whom in your personal system of relationships do you admire as someone who exhibits an inspiring authentic core? What can you learn from them?

The organizational dimension

Over the years we have found that people and groups we work with begin to understand what it means to be a responsible leader when they see themselves as a positive agent within their system, their context, rather than as a victim in it or powerless to impact it. Alfonso was one such positive agent, as we encountered earlier.

For most, this includes an organization (or teams), and we represent this by the five points on the model (see Figure 3.2) in the circle surrounding the individual in the core. We have found that people get it when we can simplify the system together with them. In many ways it becomes one lens through which they view the world. Granted, it is not the only lens that someone would use, but were an individual part of a voluntary group or community

FIGURE 3.2   The organizational dimension of responsible leadership

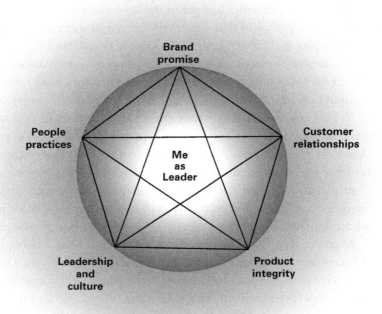

team, for example, that too would be an organizational lens with its own unique properties.

First and foremost, you will notice that these five points are linked with each other. **This is a fundamental principle: the elements of the system are connected and what happens in one impacts others.**

The second important principle is that if I am an individual leader in this system **I too am connected to each of these elements and I have a relationship with them. The nature of those relationships is what I can influence.** And it follows that these elements will have an influence on me in my role as a leader.

Let's examine each of these elements a little further.

Brand promise

To begin with, this book is not primarily about how businesses or organizations go about clarifying their brand or brand values, although clearly that process is integral to shaping the organizational culture, and hopefully one that is focused on responsible leadership. Many marketing agencies and consultancies do great work helping with this process. Nonetheless, if we assume that the organization has put in the hard yards and clarified what it collectively stands for, and that this is represented in some important statements, principles and behaviours that model the brand, then what becomes vital is the degree to which leaders in the organization have inculcated the brand into their day-to-day actions as leaders. When travelling for business, I have found that my favoured hotels spend a lot of time developing their brand. What I am interested in is how a hotel actually does its core business of hospitality and the degree to which there is some consistency of experience. The Marriott hotel group is now a global giant with hotels catering for all levels of budget and expectation. What I have noticed is the importance that Marriott places on communicating to its customers its heritage, its values and some bold claims. One such is that it encourages all staff to meet or exceed a customer's need before asking for permission from senior management, wherever they can. I have personal experience of this being enacted and it leaves me trusting them to deliver against my expectations. The brand promise gives permission to leaders and staff alike to act, knowing that in almost all cases (presumably there will be some exceptions) they will be supported by management. This is an example of a brand enabling its leaders at all levels. As a responsible leader, I am more likely to embrace the values, the heritage, the culture – the promise – and align my actions to it if it makes sense to me and I feel that I can also enhance the brand through my actions.

Contrarily, I have worked in organizations that shall remain anonymous in which it is evident that managers and leaders are distrusting of executive motives and actions and whose behaviours are misaligned with the brand promise. For example, a business that espouses ethical behavioural practices on the one hand while openly fostering overly competitive targeting for sales people leaves itself open to brand risk. In the utilities sector in the UK this has recently been exposed, as energy providers have had their sales practices shown up for being 'sharp' at best and dishonest at worst. Deceiving customers in the quest for sales has been identified as common across almost the whole sector, it seems. Customer trust has been undermined and leaders and managers have been left grappling with incongruence between what is stated in corporate publications and what is really measured and valued by executives. As Marriott states on its website, 'How we do business is as important as the business we do.'

Reflections

- To what extent are you as a leader fully inspired by, proud of and bought into your organization's brand promise?

- Is it clear to you how you can enhance your organization's brand through your actions as a leader?

- How would you describe the relationship that you have with the brand and those who are at the top of the organization?

Customer relationships

Someone once said to me that the existence of an idea does not always equal the existence of a market, and the existence of a market does not always equal the existence of a customer. To be a wise and responsible leader means both to recognize the significance of the customer relationship *and* to cherish it, to nurture it, to steward it, to deepen it, to celebrate it.

When I work with groups on this topic, I often invite them to imagine what it is that the customer wants from me as a leader, and typically the groups respond with delivery of promise, keen pricing, availability and responsiveness, among other things. When we question what this means and ask them to describe the relationship that needs to exist between customers and me, we tap into words such as respect, trust, care, concern, generosity, even affection. These are even more powerful and requiring of the responsible leader. They require me to draw deeply on my inner strength and to be determined when faced with challenges to that relationship.

We saw in the previous chapter how such a passion for customers drives Gareth. For others, it can simply be the little things that illustrate and illuminate the customer relationship. One example is the John Lewis Partnership, a UK-based retailer that is structured as a partnership in which all its staff are owners and are empowered to, indeed expected to, live their brand and passion for their customers. A colleague of mine recounts how he once visited a John Lewis store as he was researching coffee machines – the fancy ones that require capsules and produce great coffee. He goes on to say that he was baulking at the cost of these when he was approached by an assistant in the store who inquired if he needed help. When he explained what he was looking for but was reluctant to pay that price, the assistant told him that she had a display model that he could have for a more agreeable price. Done! The assistant then realized that there was a problem. There was no box for it, she said, but she took the time to work out a solution and returned with a starter kit of capsules and a box. More to the point, many people are deeply affectionate towards that particular retailer and tell others about its approach to customers and how it has successfully inculcated customer value in all its people. It is not surprising that it outperforms many other retailers and that people genuinely love working there.

A further point to make here is that as a responsible leader, I can choose my customers, just as they can choose me and my business. Within a systemic view, there may be types of businesses that, were I to do business with them, would contravene my values, perhaps damage my brand and cause misalignment for my people. Not wishing to get into deep water about this, I will draw simply on the examples that were highlighted in the press for HSBC when it became clear that it had been inadvertently acting as bankers for drug dealers and dictators. It was hauled before the US authorities and forced to pay huge fines while also changing its risk management procedures, wholesale. Some people were dismissed and a great deal of money, time and energy was needed to remedy the situation. I know that many people across that bank will have been deeply upset by the revelations that diminished their brand and undermined their daily efforts. Senior leaders were clearly contrite.

My point here is that it is almost impossible in the modern globalized world to ensure total compliance and perfect alignment. HSBC is a giant business operating in scores of territories around the world. Nonetheless, it is important to try to be seen to take action when things are not as they should be. Being intentional about customer relationships and being mindful of the ripples that these have across the wider system is the mark of the responsible organization and leader. This applies in all sectors. Patient voice for a hospital is critical to take into account. Parents and students in a school or university, the same; similarly, residents and citizens for a city authority.

Reflections

- What would (or do) your customers say about you and your organization?

- To what extent do your customers have a real affection for you and your organization based on trust, reliability, mutual respect and understanding?

- How do you foster and maintain a depth of relationship with your customers that withstands difficulties or tough times?

- As a leader, how do you model for your people responsible leadership in your dealings with customers, past, present and future?

People practices

When we invite clients to consider what their employees want from them as responsible leaders, there is a remarkable consistency of responses. Words like inspiration, support, coaching, development, stretch, honest feedback, valuing what I do, fighting for us and backing us up in discussions with senior people, interest in me and understanding of me as a person. This is not surprising at all, as these are fundamental to us all and are at the core of how we get our self-esteem. I should add that words like a decent, fair wage and flexible working practices also nearly always occur.

When we probe a little deeper and ask what it is that the responsible leader wants from his or her people, again we find consistency in the responses. As leaders we want commitment, loyalty, feedback, ideas, contributions from our teams.

And then we enquire about what it is that will be needed for the relationships with our people to work well. The answers are always the same: trust, respect, care, appreciation, honesty, decency, listening and understanding.

This is not surprising, but is reassuring. For without forcing the issue, when we as people are presented with these simple enquiries – often in the form of a high-energy constellation activity standing and looking each other in the face – we access strong emotional forces deep in our brains and we bypass our cognitive processes, by and large. And it is these deeper forces that are at work in the modern world of leading responsibly. As we saw in the previous chapter, the expectations of workforces are changing, which means that for those called to lead responsibly, it is increasingly important to ask these questions and to pay attention to mindsets and practices concerning people.

An investment bank asked me to design and facilitate some workshops to tackle people management skills development. The drivers for this work included some poor feedback in a staff survey (interestingly this, among other things, is nearly always a cause for requests for leadership programmes) and a realization on the part of senior leaders that something needed to be done. The larger cultural issues we will deal with more specifically in Part 2, but for the moment I want to highlight one conversation that emerged. As we explored with the primary client what we should cover and how, I mentioned that what we knew about what motivates people includes the degree to which they feel that their boss is interested in them and cares for them as a person. I was then advised that I should not use the word 'care' in this context as investment bankers were highly transactional in their approach to people. I would be laughed out of the room. Startled, I reminded my client that I thought I was dealing with 'human beings, not machines' and that all human beings, whether investment bankers or charity aid workers, are fundamentally the same in what we need and look for to help us function. Yes, but this is different, he went on.

To cut a longer conversation short, we proceeded with the work and although I agreed to remove the actual word 'care' from a particular slide, when the group discussion got going in the pilot event the delegates (mostly men) acknowledged without prompting that when they felt genuinely cared for they enjoyed their work more. Thereafter, we overtly referenced care as a factor in people management – even in the fast-paced world of investment banking.

For me, this raised a key principle of responsible leadership and especially so in this model, namely the need to challenge assumed wisdom and thinking to get beneath the surface and find what is incontrovertible. This means that to lead responsibly means to pay attention to and focus intentionally on *how* I am leading just as much as what and where I am leading. Furthermore, it is not just about the processes surrounding people management, such as performance management, reward or promotions per se (although clearly these are important), but more about the underpinning principles and values. Much of the energy around people engagement nowadays has recognized this and most staff surveys ask questions around the degree to which my boss or leaders inspire me, take an interest in me and are people that I can respect.

A word about international implications. In our experience working in different countries, the principles that we have identified hold true everywhere. However, what is unavoidable is that local culture has a major impact on the degree to which some of these principles and people practices are evidenced clearly. For example, in Latin America and South America, people tend to be vocal and passionate, which translates into pretty frank and honest discussions with their bosses. In North America, surprisingly, there is usually more of a compliant reaction to responsible leadership in practice that translates into more of an acceptance of status and hierarchy so long as it comes with a heart. In my experience, in Asia the picture is mixed. In China and similar cultures, including Japan, the cultural norms around deference and respect are often so powerful that we have found conversations about people engagement hard work. That said, the younger generations in the workforce are beginning to challenge established paradigms and becoming more requiring of their leaders. In Africa, the leadership paradigm is very strongly directive and positionally powerful. Sadly, this often results in controlling and dominating behaviours. We are hopeful of subtle change here, although it will take time.

Everywhere, as you might expect, the potential for bullies, dictators, despots and so on exists and I for one have many examples of such people that I will not mention here as it serves only to cause us to focus on the negative. Everywhere too, however, the potential for thoughtful, mindful and responsible people leadership is evident.

Reflections

- How do you ensure that a healthy dialogue takes place between leaders and staff in your teams and organization?

- How can you help your people see the interconnectedness of their roles within the wider system so that they too embrace a responsible leadership mindset?

- To what extent is the relationship that you have with your team one in which there is openness, respect, mutual support, stretch and development?

Product integrity

When I am asked about responsible leadership and which companies and organizations are exemplars, I tend to be guarded in my response. I believe that there are some businesses that are trying hard and doing their best, often making small steps forward against a tide of cynicism that says you are not doing enough. This journey will take time. One business that is trying to raise its game is Marks & Spencer (M&S). In the subsequent case study, we focus on how M&S is changing its perspectives on products and services through its 'Plan A' initiative (Marks & Spencer Group plc, 2007). Another is Unilever, the global consumer goods manufacturer. Both have been and are being led by individuals who see the bigger picture of responsible leadership, and both companies recognize that how they integrate their product narrative with their wider corporate narrative is crucial.

So what do we mean by product integrity? This is both a macro and a micro issue, as is the whole of our responsible leadership model. At a macro level, product integrity is about how the business's processes for sourcing, producing and delivering products and services align behind a holistic and responsible vision. For M&S, this is about how it can make its products compliant with its ambitious 'Plan A' goals, which involve a close examination of the value chain and supply chain to ensure that all parties are on message and supporting the vision. Unilever has a similar approach and it is also about how it manufactures and distributes locally in ways that adhere to its principles of sustainability, stewardship and provision of life essentials across the world. For Waitrose (the food arm of the John Lewis Partnership) it involves paying suppliers around the world a fair price that is often more than other supermarket chains will pay to ensure a strong and mutually beneficial relationship.

At an individual level, whether as a leader or not, the responsible agenda requires us to ask questions, first about how we understand what our products and services provide, how they have been created and how they are delivered to customers, and secondly, how we can make ethical and right choices that we can own. Finally, as responsible leaders we have the opportunity to explore imaginative choices and decisions around services and products that enhance our brand, deliver value to our customers and make us feel proud of what we are doing.

By way of a rather dramatic example at a macro level are the tragic events that surrounded the Deepwater Horizon Gulf of Mexico oil platform catastrophe of 2010. Without going into all the details, what became clear during the years of recriminations that followed the disaster was that BP, which operated the facility, had given control of it to other parties, including Transocean and Haliburton, and that in the quest for cost management BP had lost sight of its values and allowed poor safety management practices to go unchecked. What ensued was an unfortunate succession of blame and accusation, not helped by the then BP CEO, Tony Hayward, admitting that he wanted his life back amid the world's shock and dismay, and the local catastrophe unfolding for the citizens of the southern United States. Subsequently, BP has admitted its mistakes and has accepted responsibility for a litany of shortcomings. Hayward was forced to resign and BP's share price took a massive hit as it was faced with huge financial penalties. Hopefully also for us all, the oil and gas industry will collectively learn about the need for responsible leaders to be courageous and call out poor practices when they see them (it was reported that some employees had expressed concerns ahead of the disaster). The drive for partnerships and collaborations to reduce costs and overheads is not in itself bad. Waitrose, Unilever and M&S are examples of businesses getting this more right than wrong (at the time of writing), so it is down to the leadership operating in these businesses and given to the relationships to ensure mutual respect and genuine collective ownership of responsibility for the whole process.

Reflections

- To what extent are you confident that your products and services are aligned to and reflect your vision and purpose as an organization?

- How effective are you at building strong, respectful and mutually beneficial relationships with all parties in your supply and value chain?

- What can and could you do personally to improve the integrity of your products/services value chain?

- As an individual leader, to what extent are you confident that you can and would challenge assumptions about services and products, how they are sourced, developed and delivered across the whole system?

Leadership and culture

I have purposefully left this to the end of our short exploration of the five elements of the organizational system as it is the most important point

– leaders and the way they model leadership are the single most important determinant of an organizational culture and therefore the practices and behaviours visible to all stakeholders both internal and external. And as this book is addressing how to develop a culture of responsibility, what follows from this point is very much the essence of what we need to notice.

The responsible leader acts as a master weaver of the systemic threads inside the organization into a coherent picture that reflects the vision and purpose. He or she also connects the organization to the larger system beyond. Finally, the truly responsible organization cultivates this attitude of responsibility at all levels through well-distributed leadership. So whether the responsible leader is the CEO or a team leader in a retail department or production site, these principles apply.

Occasionally when I work with groups I use a straightforward activity that involves placing some simple words on the floor and then asking people to gather around the single word that *they like best* when they think of a leader. Typically, people avoid words like 'dictator', 'autocrat', 'controller'. Some are drawn, as you might expect, to words like 'visionary', 'strategist', 'driving force', even 'hero'. A few deliberately and courageously choose words like 'navigator', 'storyteller', 'steward', 'bridge-builder', 'peacemaker'. Occasionally I have had one or two choose 'servant' or 'enabler'. During the discussions that follow, it is fascinating to explore people's mental models of leaders, often shaped by their experiences of being led and being leaders. Naturally, not just one word is *right* and perspectives change situationally. However, when we then ask people to go and stand by the word that best describes how they think leaders should be to be effective in the future world, more people gravitate towards 'enabler', 'navigator', 'steward', even 'servant'. It seems that many of us have an intuitive sense that future leaders will need to be more facilitative than purely directional, more mindful of the wider picture. People always identify that leaders should be able to inspire others to act and respond. Our discussions also highlight the types of culture in which people want to work in the future – cultures of responsibility, accountability, stewardship, learning and enabling that feature language such as 'for the greater good' and 'for the long term'.

As a reminder, the core of the model is the individual leader and the relationship he or she has with the whole system and all parties in it. This includes the leadership in the organization and the culture. Such a relationship can be passive, defensive and overall negative, or it can be constructive, shaping and additive. For example, it is not uncommon for some discussions in workshops to include the phrase 'if only those at the top would...'. This can spiral further downwards into the place of blame and criticism, of denial and defeatism. I have seen and experienced it. Nothing is sadder than when motivated adults collude with each other to adopt the role of victim and powerlessness.

The role of the responsible leader is to engage with the leadership and the culture to impact, to explore, to examine, to shape, to change, to encourage, to congratulate and to challenge. This can only be done from a position of assured confidence and from a solid core. When done in this way it is very impressive, and in my experience tends to yield better outcomes through respectful dialogue.

The remainder of this book will develop these themes and provide some guidance on how to make progress on this journey.

Reflections

- When you think about your mental model of a 'leader as...', what words come to mind as those you like and which come to mind for you as likely to be more effective in the future? Why?

- How would you best describe the culture in your organization?

- How as a leader can you, might you, impact and live out (or change) the culture of your organization positively?

The wider global and local connection

As individuals we tend to operate in one or many organizational systems and these in turn operate in the wider global system, providing us as leaders with an organizational lens through which to view this wider world (see Figure 3.3). In an ideal world there would be strong alignment between our individual centre, the organizational perspective and the global context. The next few points seek to explore this.

Discovering the model

The model that we now use had its origins in East Africa in 2007. During a programme that I was developing with my colleagues for PwC, called 'Emerging Leaders', our intention was to help these talented individuals see their role as an agent for change, for good and for progress in the wider

FIGURE 3.3   Wider influences on responsible leadership

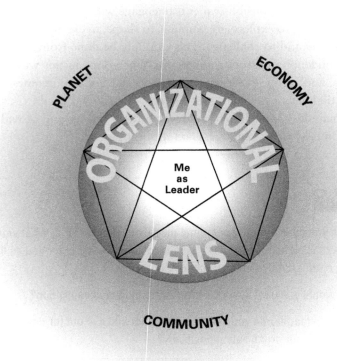

global and local context. Their lens was a PwC lens as that was the organization of which they were part, and so the model emerged that placed them in the centre and the outer ring representing the environment, society, the marketplace and their family. In a large room in a hotel in Kenya's capital Nairobi, 50 emerging leaders from around the world stood on the points of the model and expressed how they saw the system from that perspective. Energy was high. Voices were loud. Opinions were strong. It became manifestly clear that perspectives were similar yet different and in some cases poles apart. What also emerged was how passionate these young people were about ensuring that their personal journeys were aligned with an organization that saw its role in the wider world as important and benevolent. We distilled this wider context into three macro themes of **planet** – what roles the organization and leader play to respond to environmental challenges; **economy** – how they positively shape the economic forces at work;

community – how they enrich society rather than deplete it. We will focus on each of these in turn.

Planet

One such example was the debate that began around whether or not we in the UK and Europe should be buying flowers grown in Kenya's spectacular Rift Valley. Many in the room opposed the idea, citing air miles, pollution and the drive for more local production as their rationale. Following a visit to a flower farm to meet the men and women who were growing acres upon acres of roses, tulips and other flowers under totally natural conditions without the need for additional heating or lighting, some minds were beginning to shift. Then the group was taken into a laboratory compound as part of the operation in which locally trained Kenyan scientists were researching the growing in boxes of natural bugs that fed on pests that attack the flowers without damaging them – natural pesticides. Next was a visit to the packing plant where the flowers were carefully and tenderly packed into bunches, labelled with the supermarket's labelling, and then collated to be flown out that night to arrive in London or Paris or Rome in time for Christmas (our visit was in December) with a 7- or 14-day guarantee of quality. The operation was impressive, the more so because it provides employment for six thousand local East Africans along with associated housing, schooling and health care.

Returning to our base, we encouraged the participants to consider the choices faced by consumers in London supermarkets. Should they buy flowers grown in somewhat forced conditions in Holland or the Channel Islands (it was Christmas, remember) or in natural conditions in Africa? Would they know the difference? What are the social implications of each option? Is there a right answer? We soon recognized that the dilemmas were real and yet many consumers were unaware of them.

Now the questions began to revolve around what the role of the leaders should be and that of businesses such as PwC. Should businesses do more to inform customers about the whole system? Should leaders of those businesses do more to train their own people about how their roles are instrumental in shaping wider societies and communities? How can the environment be stewarded carefully while also providing livelihoods for thousands of people who otherwise would have limited opportunity for schooling and health provision? The Africans in the group were clear about the case for doing more to grow such businesses. The Americans and Europeans were, as you might imagine, thoughtful about the dilemma, framed as it was by established economies and settled paradigms. Interestingly, the delegates from Russia and China were themselves provoked to think about how this system was being played out in their still-emerging economies with all the associated growing pains.

Subsequent years have accelerated this debate on every continent and in every serious business. Now, when we buy a car we have a choice of a hybrid or zero emissions vehicle. We can buy hemp T-shirts and bamboo underwear. Energy provision is top of the political agenda as prices soar. Organizations building new headquarters are recycling heat and water to be carbon neutral, even utilizing used chip fat as fuel and minimizing footprints.

Clearly the environmental agenda (**Planet**) is being heard and progress is being made – perhaps more slowly than some would want – but the debate has shifted significantly over the early years of the new millennium. Al Gore, the former American Vice President, has done much to bring this to the forefront of our minds through his work *An Inconvenient Truth: The planetary emergency of global warming and what we can do about it* (2006), and as such has been a strong example of someone in a position of real influence who has used a voice responsibly. Perhaps at the other end of the spectrum, for a responsible leader in a small business, this can be as simple as the choice between buying recyclable paper cups for coffee rather than cheaper plastic versions.

It is clear that the environmental voice is loud and requiring of us to think and make choices. Individual purchases, journeys in our cars, heating systems, solar panels on our houses, devices to collect rainwater are all figural now in our lives. In the corporate world, choosing to have a video conference over a meeting in person is now commonplace. We believe we have saved paper by using e-mail and this may be true, although the power needed to keep hundreds of server farms running is frightening. The tensions and dilemmas are real. What is important is that as responsible leaders we are mindful of them and choiceful as best we can be.

Reflections

- How do you reflect wider global and environmental (Planet) issues in your leadership through your words and actions?
- Which organizations do you admire for doing good work for the greater good and why do you admire them?
- What can you learn from them?

Economy

Earlier in this chapter we met Alfonso, who creatively brought the outer circle of the economy and market together with the community and through his company, in this case HSBC, was able to create a virtuous alignment and deliver a powerful result for all parties. **Responsible leaders engage proactively with the forces that shape the economic landscape** and they look for ways in which their organization can influence the debate for the greater good. Nowhere is this more apparent in the modern world than in the domain of regulations and good conduct.

Recently I was privileged to meet one such leader and interview her about her perspectives on this debate. Margaret Cole was branded the chief enforcer during her time at the Financial Services Authority (FSA), the UK's regulatory body (recently rebranded as the Financial Conduct Authority), where she was instrumental in pursuing high-profile unethical and fraudulent banking cases, including several individuals for insider dealing. Now the chief legal counsel at PwC, she is forthright in her views about how responsible leadership should be outworked in the marketplace. Brought up in a working-class Catholic family in Lancashire, she attributes her moral framework to her parents and her mother in particular. Understanding of hard work and what was right for the wider good was instilled in her early years and at 17 she spent a year on a kibbutz in Israel where she experienced shared values being outworked.

It was her work on two high-profile cases in the 1990s – the collapse of BCCI and the Robert Maxwell affair – that brought her to the forefront of litigation in the public eye. She says that it was an opportunity for her to do something good for widows and orphans based on truth and justice. Over time, though, she too became disillusioned with the legal profession itself, as she saw it moving from an ethic of serving clients towards a corporate model driven by performance pressures and targets that at worst became a pressure to keep litigation going even when it was not in the client's interest to do so. Her move to the FSA was her moment to make a difference and to step up courageously, as she puts it.

In a moment of philosophical candour she says that she remains a little sceptical about the market's ability and in particular the financial services sector to self-correct and breed a new cadre of leaders who will act responsibly. As she observes astutely, few bankers are queuing up to change their reward and remuneration packages as a response to public disgust – worldwide it should be said – and step out from the group courageously. The dilemma of the choice between money and justice is proving too strong for many in that sector to reconcile, in her view. Nonetheless, she is heartened by the moves by Anthony Jenkins, appointed to be CEO at Barclays in 2012 (replacing Bob Diamond, whose track record of dealing with that particular dilemma was not strong), who has come out and openly challenged the bank's strategy around high-risk investment banking. His moves to redress the balance back to so-called core banking and reconnect with Barclays' original values is laudable and a current example of the responsible leadership model being outworked organizationally. But as Cole reminds us, culture change takes time and courage, especially when everyone else is ploughing a different furrow, apparently anyway. She goes on to reinforce her point that courage is the key: the courage to speak out and stand for something against group think, to pause and think about the genuinely right thing for the good of the wider community and system, to take a long-term view possibly at short-term personal cost. She herself has modelled responsible leadership and her infectious energy is certainly cause for hope that others will catch the spirit.

Reflections

- Honestly, to what extent do you regard your role as a leader as someone who can and should shape the wider economic system proactively for the greater good?

- What small actions (or large ones) can you take to role-model this?

- How do you connect your personal core and identity with the wider economic system?

Community

Most listed companies these days advocate that they want to do the right thing for their communities. So on that basis, our communities should be flourishing places and the positive hand of the corporation should be very evident.

This is happening increasingly. As we examined earlier, the Quakers knew the value of integrating community and business when they recognized many decades ago the link between a happy workforce and business success. The question now is: Can global businesses model something similar or should they develop another model? Are they just saying fine words to appease critics? And also, what is the role for smaller, local businesses or different models that might be emerging?

First, I believe we need to clarify what it is that we are talking about when we include 'community' in the responsible leadership model. Responsible leadership is about an active involvement in the system. It requires a positive agency mindset that is contributory and constructive. It is about engagement with and participation in. It is fundamentally 'otherish', which is to say that it balances the needs of self and the organization with the needs of others in the wider system.

Therefore, what it is *not* is a token CSR box-ticking exercise. Wayne Visser, in his excellent book *The Age of Responsibility* (Visser, 2011), charts the transition of CSR box-ticking from the age of greed, as he calls it, through the ages of philanthropy, marketing and management to the coming age of responsibility. He challenges the organizational mindset of philanthropic paternalism towards communities and suggests that what are needed are more proactive strategies that can be judged on actual social, environmental and ethical performance.

Peter Block, the business and consulting guru, has, in partnership with John McKnight, offered some radical thinking about how local communities can begin to rethink how they sustain themselves from within and draw on the abundance in their midst. Their work *The Abundant Community* (2010) fundamentally challenges the mindset difference between consumer and citizen. This is a theme that I believe is at the heart of responsible leadership. To be a citizen is to contribute and be additive, to look to grow the whole. To be a consumer is to use up, to acquire and grow the individual without considering the impact on the whole.

This thinking is crucial for our understanding of responsible leadership and being a responsible leader. So what does this look like in practice?

When I work with groups exploring the model, we spend time asking what it is that the community requires of us as leaders and organizations. Some of the key themes that emerge consistently are:

- When we consider ourselves as part of the community, we want businesses to treat us fairly and not take us for a ride. We want businesses to play by the rules and not to think themselves above the law or better than the average man in the street. This is ethical behaviour in practice.

- We also want businesses to be mindful of families and the pressure on them because of the long working hours that are demanded.

Intuitively we know that this has an impact on society. Time is a valuable currency and we sense that businesses are not acknowledging this. This is true in almost all the countries that I have worked in, although it is most present in so-called developed economies and in global businesses (often following a western template) that insist that their pervading culture is replicated wherever they operate.

- We want organizations to use resources wisely and to create employment. And, surprisingly, in pretty much every territory I've worked in, we want businesses to share wealth and invest back into society and communities generously and not just as a token gesture.

Now this might be because the topic we are exploring is responsible leadership, but equally it is at the core of us as human beings – we recognize lip service and it does not inspire us at all. Quite the opposite in fact, as we become cynical and our expectations are lowered. When this happens we find ourselves joining the corporates in a vicious and decreasing circle of reducing hope and expectation, leading to a defeatist mindset. If you don't believe me, just ask any Greek or Spaniard facing huge economic austerity, caused in their view by the government itself.

Starbucks is a company that I have already admonished for its clumsy tax accounting debacle. Like it or not, this will stick with it for many years to come. However, it is important to redress the balance, as Starbucks is a company that has tried hard over many years to promote community-oriented policies and practices. Locally, stores are encouraged to be hubs for their local communities, whether it is organizing reading groups, mother and toddler sessions or cake-making. In many respects, stores have become modern-day community centres. On a larger scale, the business has invested in creating apprenticeships in the UK and, through its Coffee and Farmer Equity scheme, has tried to support local coffee producers in Central America, Africa and beyond with training and a fair deal. Looking to the longer term, its Youth Leadership schemes are training young leaders around the world in communities that have ties with Starbucks. I admire it for having a go and holding true to Howard Shultz's vision for a vibrant company that is about individual relationships in stores and with wider communities.

If these points are true for large organizations, then we as leaders in those organizations have a responsibility to make it possible and play our part, large or small. We will address some practical responses in Part 2, but for now, I want to remind us that as a leader, we role-model behaviour.

- To what extent are you essentially a mere consumer or do you consciously add something back and invest?

- Do you expect someone else to be doing this on your behalf, or are you personally involved?

- Are you creating opportunities or merely taking out profits – how are you contributing rather than taking?

- How are you demonstrating that you value time that families and employees have together as important recharging and refreshing moments?

- How do you actively support your team members who are passionate about their involvement in their communities?

Summary

In summary, we have tried to illustrate the world of a responsible leader simply, using this model of a system in which he or she is required to lead.

At the centre is the leader himself or herself. To be effective, leaders can operate from a grounded centre that means they are:

- clear about their core identity;
- aspiring to make a significant contribution through their vision and legacy;
- aware of and content to leverage their talents and capability.

Responsible leaders see themselves impacting the organizational systems in which they operate through their positive and intentional relationships with different aspects of the system, including:

- the organizational brand;
- external customers and clients;
- internal teams, people and colleagues;
- products and services;
- leadership and culture.

Finally, the outer circle of our model represents our relationship with the interconnected world. Simply put, this can mean that we relate to this outer system through the lenses of our organizations and our own personal core. This involves:

- how we interpret the environmental agenda (**planet**) and contribute positively to shaping that agenda;

- how we as producers, traders and consumers create economic realities that liberate people and create opportunities for the greater good (**economy**);

- how as organizations we enrich society and the wider communities intentionally, so that they too can respond to the wider challenges we collectively face (**community**).

Getting these right may well be a differentiator for businesses or leaders who can attract, work with and retain great people *and* great customers.

For the emerging responsible leader, the gauntlet that has been thrown down to us is how to rise above a victim and powerless mindset to thrive in the system and impact it as a positive agent. In the next chapter we will begin to tackle how this challenge manifests itself through tensions in the system and how we can embrace these – responsibly.

Living with paradox as a responsible leader

04

> *Let go of certainty. The opposite isn't uncertainty. It's openness, curiosity and a willingness to embrace paradox, rather than choose up sides. The ultimate challenge is to accept ourselves exactly as we are, but never stop trying to learn and grow.* **(TONY SCHWARTZ)**

There is tension inherent in the systemic model that we addressed in the previous chapter. In addition, as we look to gain control of our role in the system we are exposed to more dilemmas that exert force on us as individual leaders and the system. Mastering these forces is the responsible leader's quest.

The emerging leaders that were with me in Kenya found the time spent with the poor in the slums of Nairobi deeply unsettling. Not surprisingly, they experienced the conditions as uncomfortable in the extreme – tens of thousands of people living in cramped and squalid conditions with no running water and limited access to power. Such an experience is challenging for those whose worlds are manifestly different. However, what was perhaps more interesting was the discomfort felt by most about the fact that they wanted to do something about it, to fix it, to put it right and to relieve the pressure on their consciences, and yet could do nothing there and then. Seemingly wealthy and with informational power through knowledge acquired, they were apparently powerless in the face of such inequality.

To have everything and apparently be able to do nothing of value, therein lies torment. To know what could be but feel powerless to do anything is frustration.

The debates that followed were highly charged, focusing blame on corrupt politicians and businesses in equal measure. What the group had begun to engage with was the nature of the paradox that we experience living in the 21st century. And it is this that merits further consideration as we develop our picture of responsible leadership and the responsible leader.

This chapter discusses what I believe to be three significant dilemmas present in the leading landscape today and what they mean for aspirant responsible leaders. There are certainly many more, but I have found these to be ever present in discussions:

- How can we hear when there is so much noise?
- How can we see beyond the immediate?
- How can we redefine success when we are under so much pressure to perform?

Listening to hear through the noise – cultivate serenity

Brain fatigue

Modern neuroscience is discovering that our brains are more malleable than has been traditionally thought to be the case. This is encouraging as we live longer and promises a more fulfilled second half of life for many. But the same neuroscience is also revealing that **our brains are consumers of energy and can become fatigued when overused**. This is particularly the case when we are being required to make countless decisions each day. Our brains engage the pre-frontal cortex to make even the smallest of decisions about opening an e-mail in the same way that would be the case if we were deciding to move house or job. This requires energy, whereas a habitual pattern is deeply engrained in the inner parts of our brains – the hippocampus – and has become learnt such that our brains respond automatically, requiring far less energy consumption.

It is an unavoidable truth that those of us alive today have access to more information than most of our ancestors combined, and it's at the tips of our fingers. It is not uncommon for many people to access e-mails, Twitter feeds and social networking relationships as soon as they wake. By the time people reach their place of work they will have been bombarded with scores of decisions, all draining their brain's resources. Typically then, their first actions will be to open more e-mails, each of which requires a decision.

What is going on? Imagine trying to have a conversation with someone in a large conference room with so much background noise that it renders hearing, thinking, responding and making oneself heard above the noise exhausting. You may have been there. Visualize also trying to have a conversation on your phone in a city-centre street next to a roadside engineer drilling through the pavement while an ambulance passes by, sirens aloud. It is tiring and hugely ineffective. The potential for miscommunication is huge.

When we use the systemic constellation activity with groups (we introduced this in the previous chapter), we often place an individual in the centre of the model and have all the surrounding stakeholders express their demands and concerns simultaneously. The cacophony is made worse when we encourage stakeholders to raise their voices, if they do not believe they are being heard. Regularly we find that the individuals burst into laughter at the absurdity of the scenario. Often we encounter people who recognize this as their reality and are shocked when they accept that they tolerate it – daily. Many confess to being tired of it, both physically and emotionally.

The illusion of busyness

In the midst of this noise, the leader is required to make judgements, to evaluate, to persuade, to inspire, to appease, to relate – the list goes on. And the reaction is a metaphorical laugh of resignation, or, and this is far more common in reality, a complete denial that it is happening and a belief that by simply opening up to more information, the leader will inevitably be more effective. This is an illusion.

By way of an example, I was called to a meeting with a client in its head office building (a 40-storey tower block – this is important information) at which I was asked to present a report of findings. Four people were to attend, plus myself. When I arrived I was shown to the meeting room on the 35th floor where I waited for my clients. I was five minutes early as I wanted to prepare myself well for this session and get familiar with the room. One of the clients arrived five minutes after the due start time, two more a few minutes later and one arrived 15 minutes later – none having given any warning of the delay. The meeting proceeded, but with five minutes to go before the scheduled end, the man who had been 15 minutes late (a senior department head) announced that he was going to have to leave as he had another meeting starting on the hour on the 10th floor and that it would take him 10 minutes to negotiate the two different lifts to reach that floor. I had been aware that he had zoned out of the session several minutes before and that his contributions throughout had been rushed, ill thought through and, if I am being honest, unprofessional. I kept the scraps of paper upon which he scribbled a model as it took me a while to decipher them. This was a man who was out of control, enslaved to a diary that he was clearly not managing and, more to the point, not interested in a mutually beneficial conversation with me, his supplier. I felt used and valueless. Clearly, he thought he was being effective and appearing important. The truth was that his world was so full of noise that he was delusional about his effectiveness. I was not surprised to hear that his role was made redundant some months later, as he had evidently not been as influential as he had hoped.

If you are reading this and recognizing it as possibly true of you or your organization, I would not be surprised in the slightest. I encounter this kind of behaviour frequently and I have fallen prey to this illusion on many occasions in a previous role. But it is not responsible leadership. It is merely responding to the loudest voice or the next one.

So how is the responsible leader to rise above the noise and the conflicting demands on his or her time and energy?

Focus to create serenity

Daniel Goleman's recent work *Focus: The Hidden Driver of Excellence* (2013) draws this out as he identifies that it is the degree to which leaders focus their attention that has a profound impact on effectiveness. Goleman highlights **the importance of focusing on self to begin with and in particular honing skills and techniques around self-control and self-awareness.** In our experience this is becoming critical now for responsible leaders. Given the pace of life, the proliferation of information and the public exposure of decisions and judgements, leaders that already (and will in the future) inspire commitment, create assurance and make things happen have a kind of serenity that allows them to pause amid the noise and to identify where to put their attention. They act as a guide through the maelstrom because they can rise above it and see a path or a priority.

In the world of elite sport, it is common for supreme sportsmen and women to describe key moments in games in slow motion where they can perceive a movement of a ball or an opponent and then evaluate their position and response in microseconds. This is clearly a natural talent, but there is something else that differentiates the best from the rest (many of us can play many sports but simply do not reach that level of ability).

Most elite sports people have developed the ability to focus and to block out distraction. Great tennis players move serenely about the court, seemingly oblivious at times to the myriad of distractions around them.

However, in the world of commerce and organizational life, it is very common for people to be working on their e-mails and phones while trying to participate in a meeting. In times when judgements are needed quickly to demonstrate agility, that does not mean that as humans we can make multiple judgements simultaneously. In fact, science proves that multitasking, when each task requires analysis and weighing of options, is nigh on impossible. We need to give each one clear attention, as they use similar amounts of the energy in our pre-frontal cortex. It is possible to multitask when one or more of the tasks is habitual and routine and requires no conscious thought, for example travelling on the subway to work, but how many of our interactions with others are like that? A large percentage of the business decisions we make on our own at our desks require some analysis and careful thought. Without attention we open ourselves to risk and poor decision-making.

Add to this the fact that most decisions we make are based significantly on our emotional state and responses and you can see the potential for poor judgement. Without paying attention to emotions deeper in our and others' being, it is easier to respond in haste. How many people have sent an e-mail they regretted sending because they were angered by something, then distracted or time-pressured?

We run assessment events for clients and it becomes evident very early who in the group is able to pay attention to all that is being said, the nuances of the discussions and the possible pitfalls. These are the people who do not constantly respond to their phones at every incoming e-mail or text. Such a mindset is a core part of judgement as a leader.

How do leaders develop this ability? Like most things, it is a combination of mindset and practice. In Part 2 we will explore this in more detail, but at this point, by way of practical suggestions:

- First, as we have affirmed before, know yourself, your aims and goals and how these translate into the *few* things that will be important for you to achieve long-term fulfilment. This is foundational.

- Second, develop skills to listen, and listen deeply. This is critical. Listening means pausing (often literally) to notice deeper reactions and allow intuition and insight to emerge; listening to self, to the spoken and unspoken, to emotion and intuitive (even soulful) reactions; beginning to recognize and distinguish between helpful and unhelpful contributions, so that this becomes second nature; noticing language that resonates and is congruent.

- Third, develop the ability and practice of stepping out of and/or rising above the maelstrom to observe it through a series of different lenses and from different perspectives. Be disciplined about this.

- Finally, act, decisively. Re-enter the system and move your energy and attention in your chosen direction, quickly and calmly.

This dilemma of needing to deal with the noise of the conflicting stakeholder demands and excess communication, while trying to create and model a calm serenity amid the busyness and cacophony, is the first aspect of the responsible leader's paradox.

Reflections

- Honestly appraise yourself against the descriptions above – are you operating under the illusion of busyness? What traps do you fall prey to?

- What can you do to be more focused when you need to be and to give proper attention to the things, situations and people that warrant it?

- If you were demonstrating more serenity in your daily life, what would be the benefit to you and others around you?

Looking for and seeing beyond while dealing with the immediate

Chess grandmasters apparently see the game as a complete unfolding scenario, having started on an inevitable course from the earliest moves. World-class snooker players plan several moves ahead so that they can control the cue ball meticulously, to within a centimetre, to be in the correct position to build the break. Both, of course, also have to focus on the immediate move in front of them to avoid making a careless error. Slalom canoeists who ride the whitewater rapids not only have to deal with the immediate stroke but also have to be looking ahead to position the boat in the right water to navigate the best route through the rapids. They have learnt how to read the eddies, to notice the subtle changes in the movement of the water, and they then take a calculated guess as to what might present dangers or a safe course – all in a split second.

These examples illustrate the dilemma of seeing beyond while acting skilfully in the moment.

Scan widely; challenge assumptions

We have found that a key orientation for people trying to lead well in turbulent times is to be scanning their world proactively and developing a kind of peripheral vision. When I am asked about what this means in practice, I often challenge individuals and groups to spend some time walking through the streets of a busy city and simply observe people who are making their way around it, but typically these days with their heads down, focused on a mobile phone, or with a far-away gaze as they are engaged with a call they are making while walking. It is characteristically only tourists who have their eyes open wide and their heads up – naturally so, as they have come to see, to look and to take in.

And yet, as business people or leaders in organizations, to what extent do we actively allow ourselves time and space to 'take in' what is around us? To what extent do we look beyond the obvious and the immediate data for the unexpected or unlikely? Do we consult widely and quickly with people who might not naturally be in our sphere of work? Where do we look for answers – to old ways and practices or to new sources of inspiration?

One of the reasons for developing the leadership programme for PwC, which I referred to in the previous chapter, was to encourage in emerging leaders a curiosity and deeper thinking about the world and its complexities. Our aim was to encourage participants to engage with the dilemma so that they could be co-creators of the way forward. This was driven by a distinct challenge to an assumption that had been made for many years previous, namely that the leaders of the future for the business would be easy to identify and would come from an established pool of people who were already well set on a career path.

Having challenged the leaders of the business on this point and entered into a constructive debate, it became clear that the leaders of tomorrow might not resemble the leaders of today in so many ways. Indeed, if they did, the business might not be able to compete as effectively, given the changing world and associated complexity. A fresh approach to developing talent within the business was born and the business was enlightened enough to see that this would take several years to work through to maturity, if ever.

At the same time, it was important to keep the business model going and not to demotivate those people who were further along the development path, as they represented the core of the business that would still be necessary to keep it successful in the short term. It will be a key priority for the responsible leader of a business in the future to consistently challenge assumptions about the war for talent and where their short-term and long-term people resources will be found.

As we have already seen, a track record of success in benign conditions, or even growth conditions, will not necessarily guarantee similar achievements in the opposite or different conditions. One of the reasons that the financial services industry has been so slow to respond to public outrage following the crash of 2008 has been the apparent ease with which the same people have simply been recycled around the industry. Even more disturbing is the complaint that we hear about the need to pay extravagant bonuses to individuals who may or may not be performing extraordinarily, simply because everyone else is paying them, and if one institution did not then all the good people would simply move to those that were paying bonuses. Whether this is a war for talent is debatable. Surely such an argument is the realm of mercenaries who are simply in the game for the quickest dollar rather than for the responsible, longer-term sustainable future of an economy and society. These include the same people who presided over the practices and behaviours that precipitated the original crash. It begs the question: What do we mean by talent and what do we expect from such people now and in the future? To what extent do we want a workforce of such mercenaries?

To first notice and then challenge assumptions is a key skill to master the dilemma.

Ripples

This brings me to the second aspect of seeing beyond – looking for and noticing ripples. **Once we acknowledge that we live in an interconnected world, it becomes clear that most of our choices have impact elsewhere or on others.** For example, if I buy a hybrid car I hope that I am having an impact on the environment through a reduction in fuel consumption and a change in emissions. However, as I think further and see further, I could also be having an impact on the lives of asthma sufferers in a small way. I could be furthering science and technology discoveries by supporting research and encouraging fresh thinking. I could be contributing to societal transformation as I educate my children into new patterns of thinking about consumption. The concept of a ripple is a simple one. Accepting that my decisions and actions *will* reach far beyond the immediate here and now invites me to be more considerate.

In my work as an executive coach and people developer, I encounter many people each year who are attentive to me and what I might be saying or advocating. Many years ago I realized that it was important for me to treat these interactions as unique leadership moments that might (or might not) have profound impact on the individuals or groups I was dealing with. More importantly, I accept that I may never know what the longer-term outcomes might be for the person and the people in his or her world, but because of this fact, I have a duty to tread carefully, to act generously, to model authenticity and to trust for a positive outcome somewhere and at some time.

As leaders, once we adopt this mindset, it releases us to enjoy each inter- action in the moment. The stories about how thoughtfully Nelson Mandela treated all those around him are myriad, from the occasion when he invited the driver of a visiting dignitary to share the intimate lunch he was having with that leader, to the times he met with celebrities to court their favour. He was masterful in knowing that he could further his nation's course by supporting the global war on poverty or AIDS through backing a famous rock star or film star. Each party's credibility within the global community was raised. It is also beyond question now, after his death, that the way he interacted with the guards during his imprisonment led many to see him in a different light and to support his presidency and attempts to transform the fledgling nation. He understood consequences and ripples. How many of us working in the field of leadership development reference his approach as we seek to inspire and enable future leaders? We can only hope that young men and women in Africa continue to draw inspiration from his life as they shape their future.

Watching Mandela pay attention in the moment to someone and to remember the details about people must have been impressive. Moreover, think for a moment about the learning that so many will have taken from that simple interaction: how they will tell the story; how they might treat their teams in their organizations now and in the future. In an interview published in *Beautifully Said Magazine*, in July 2012, the poet Maya Angelou was famously quoted as saying: 'I've learned that people will forget what you said, people will forget what you did, but people will never forget how you made them feel.' A powerful lesson for leaders.

In business, decisions may well be more significant. Whether to close a factory or open one? Whether to continue to invest in a project, or shelve it? Whether to do business with a particular client, or to walk away with integrity intact? Whether to call out bad behaviour and blow the whistle, or remain silent?

An employee who chooses to highlight unethical behaviour, as has happened more frequently of late in the public sector, the private sector, the military and politics, responds courageously to their conscience. The ripples from their action will be far reaching, even as far as changing culture, as has happened in the UK's National Health Service and the US military. Similarly, persuading a board to forgo short-term profits in order to create jobs and regenerate a local economy takes courage in the face of shareholder demands.

Consider the ripple effect of a leader accepting responsibility for a genuine error and taking steps to redress the impact. Such was not the case with the previously mentioned BP Deep Water Horizon disaster, and the negative ripples were, and continue to be, far reaching for that business.

Practical suggestions

- Cultivate and practise active and constant engagement with stakeholders to scan widely – customers, staff, markets, politicians, for example – to notice the patterns and the questions that these raise. For example, only by dialoguing with Generations Y and Z will it be possible to begin to see the world as they will see it and to earn respect and trust to co-create with them.

- Be open to and actively promote the challenge of previously held assumptions, balancing analytical thinking with intuition in the moment.

- Introduce habits of thinking about consequences and ripples. For example, the Iroquois Indians believed that any decision should be taken mindful of the impact that it would have on up to seven generations ahead. Such thinking has found its way into the environmental sustainability movements. Whether seven generations is too far for an organization or a business is open to question, but the concept is nonetheless worthy. As leaders, shouldn't we consider the impact of our choices on our teams even after we have moved on? Shouldn't we be more proactive and imaginative in our thinking about the type of talent and capability our organization will need several years ahead?

Redefining success

How a leader's performance is measured and aligned to organizational priorities is an important lever in creating a culture of responsibility. For individual leaders, though, there is a more fundamental challenge and this in turn shapes the organizational response: how to be clear about what success looks like and how to consider this over the long term while also delivering against short-term expectations of stakeholders. In many ways, this dilemma lies at the root of responsible leadership.

In the mid-1970s, free market economists and academics began to seize upon the theories of Milton Friedman and others that espoused that a company should exist for the benefit of its shareholders and its owners.

This became the dominant business theory during the 1980s and the inexorable rise of free market capitalism so championed by Reagan and Thatcher in particular. Subsequent politicians across many parts of the world based their economic strategies on the certainty of tax-revenue levels from commercial profits and the seemingly unstoppable rise of living standards and consumerism in the West and East alike. Growth and shareholder value mattered at all costs. Financial products and balance sheets became more complicated, indeed so complicated that only those people dealing with discrete parts of the design would be able to understand the detail. People at the top of many businesses now freely admit that they did not understand what was being traded as derivative products. Yet few people raised any eyebrows at the high leverage levels beginning to appear in some banks in particular. Leverage is the ratio of assets to equity, that is, how much capital is held to cover any loans held that go bad. In the case of Lehman Brothers, for example, at the time of the crash in 2008, this was close to 32 : 1. Since then, capital adequacy rules have been introduced to set a limit much closer to 10 : 1.

Growth, size and profits had blinded wisdom, it appeared. Business schools' programmes focused on the financial disciplines and outcomes, and although there were components of modules that acknowledged other drivers of effectiveness, largely this was in service of the financial nirvana of constant growth and return on capital. Not surprisingly, we all played along as the stock markets yielded returns for individuals and returns to corporate investors such as pension funds.

Such measures are not bad. They are an essential part of good management and stewardship, principles that are important for our study of responsible leadership. However, despite the best efforts of Robert Kaplan and the balanced scorecard approach introduced in the 1990s to redress the imbalance, it would be hard to argue that during the period from the mid-1980s to the mid-2000s there was anything other than a primary focus on rewarding those who delivered the numbers.

Success in the future: the dilemma of agility

Given our working hypothesis that the future may not be a simple, gradual iterative change from the past but more of a revolution or at best a rapid evolution, it suggests that leaders will need to recalibrate their view of success and how to achieve it. Straight-line growth may not be the real measure of success in the new volatile, uncertain, complex and ambiguous (VUCA) world.

If agility and responsiveness are going to be important to sustain the existence of an enterprise or organization, then success could be defined in terms of speed of ideas to product. A strong case is that it will be portfolio agility that impacts performance, that is, the ability to introduce new products or services and to kill redundant ones quickly to avoid wasted effort. This suggests embracing a short-term fleet-of-foot mindset in order to endure. But as we have highlighted, a narrow short-term focus tends also to blinker decision-making.

Structural agility will be critical. As we have seen, large infrastructures slow decision-making. It follows that the organizations with flexible structures and workforces able to play different roles dependent on the tactics needed will be more likely to grab the moment. And yet we suspect that constant restructuring creates more of an illusion of progress than progress itself. Moreover, it serves to destabilize and disengage the workforce in many instances and in so doing reduce productivity, which in turn then suggests that further restructuring could be needed. And so a cycle of paralysing introspection develops while the world moves quickly forward.

A potential requirement for leadership agility follows. Leaders who know their strengths and shortcomings, and can recognize the leadership moments to act or not act, will be in demand. We shall see in Part 2 that this is easier said than done, however, as the temptation to stay on as the leader who has built an organization when one should step aside is a strong one. Equally, it is a brave leader who repositions a deliverer of the numbers who cannot retain good people.

Furthermore, if (and it is a big if) we are more suspicious of growth as an ultimate goal, it might follow that businesses that do become large and dominant could well attract doubters and critics sooner than they would wish. How long will it be before our global love affair with new hi-tech companies such as Google or Samsung begins to dull when as a global village we decide that they control too much of our lives through their portfolio agility? As human beings we like to think that we have the power to decide while also valuing ease. But when our trust is called into question, the affront outweighs the ease more often than not.

Ensuring the consistency of message and approach for such large multinationals has traditionally been difficult, with few businesses able to do it well. Apple and Unilever are good exemplars but, as we have seen, others have set out with good intentions and fallen down when one part of the empire has stepped out of line.

If agility and responsiveness lead to diversity, this is a good thing. It will be interesting to see the extent to which organizations and individual leaders stretch their imagination around what success could also mean.

For example, an organization that is known as a developer of talent for the wider global community may not grow its financial asset base, instead aiming for growth in terms of its reputation and the value of its human potential. It is not uncommon in the world of sport for a club never to win major honours but to sustain its position through an outstanding academy that identifies and develops future stars who are sold on to the major league teams. Success in this case can be the extent to which the club acknowledges its core purpose and heritage, and outworks it conscientiously. Could some businesses learn from this model?

And what about parts of our societies and communities for which measuring success is proving problematic? Consider education. League tables for business schools and universities exist, and embrace not only academic grading results but also quality of student experience, contributions to research and the ease with which graduates secure employment. Such a diverse range of outcomes is healthy and drives quality and, importantly, the ways in which the institution focuses its priorities. It is also distinctly possible for the smallest of universities to compete with the biggest. However, with schools, such measurement is still in its infancy and is the subject of much division. Attempts to balance the debate around the problems with inner-city 'underprivileged' areas versus the elite and 'privileged' have stuttered on the grounds of purely focusing on academic results.

In the health sector, success is measured on a range of indicators, some primitive and some more helpful. Waiting times in triage is for many an important indicator of efficiency. And yet, one could argue that a hospital is dealing with both the physical and emotional well-being of its users, and therefore, the notion of being treated as a number on a scale of efficiency seems to address neither of these needs well. Clearly, if I have cause to attend the emergency department, I want to be seen as quickly as possible. But if this is not possible (and there can be many good reasons why this may be the case), the degree to which my experience is nonetheless tolerable becomes important. This will depend on how the staff view their roles. Are they to be operators of a machine in which the input raw material is an injured body to fix, or are they to be dealing with someone's anxiety and confusion? One requires a process, the other a responsible choice. And, of course, both are necessary for the system to operate well.

A client of mine recently invited me into his business to help with a challenge. He runs a company that deals with the provision of care services to a population, often elderly or housebound, and his business operates in the confused space that is between the public sector and the private sector. He is charged with running his business in profit but operates with one major owner – in this case the local authority whence the business was floated. His dilemma is that many of his staff team are struggling with change and the need to adopt new working practices. Many are trapped in old bureaucracy mindsets. Some are worried that what they perceived as a caring business has been taken over by the financial monitors, thereby diluting the real essence of what they are providing. His belief is that if his people were happier, service standards would follow and people would be more able to think for themselves rather than relying on old procedures and rules. But how to develop happiness and how to measure it? Is happiness an indication of success?

Returning to an early discussion, engagement is now a buzzword and organizations are working hard to find ways to connect better with their people. Sadly, for many this still involves measuring processes such as the frequency of a performance review or attendance on training courses. We shall explore in Part 2 what organizations can do beyond this, but the important principle that leads to this dilemma is that the responsible leader has to balance his or her own personal view of success with the organizational perspective and that of each member of the team or organization, and with how important stakeholders in the wider system will be defining success.

The following case study about the UK retailer Marks & Spencer (M&S) illustrates an expanded definition of success beyond the retailer's normal short-term sales measures. The temptation for leaders in large organizations can be to rely on paradigms that they have used over the years or that have been accepted as 'the way things are measured around here'. As the revolution gathers pace, it will be the ability to look wider for models of success and different paradigms that will set responsible leaders apart. For as they do so, they will be able to connect better with stakeholders and inspire their people through a compelling narrative.

Practical suggestions

- As you review your key performance indicators (KPIs), consider the extent to which indicators that measure 'how things are achieved' rather than 'what is achieved' are given equal weighting and that this is clear to all stakeholders.

- Consider where you can look for alternative perspectives on success across all facets of society and communities, including the not-for-profit sector (where typically there is less overt focus on numbers).

- Ensure that tough questions about agility are asked at management and board sessions more often. Questions such as: What shall we discontinue or stop? What prevents us from making decisions more quickly? Why do we consider restructuring as the primary route to enabling agility? What behavioural patterns are we enslaved by and keep repeating?

- Examine the organizational culture and how it might trap people and leaders into modelling the wrong behaviours or release them into responsible behaviours.

CASE STUDY   M&S – towards becoming the world's most sustainable retailer

Retailers have by the very nature of their business a short-term perspective. Year-on-year comparative results are the foodstuff of the business pages in the UK press and this is replicated the world over. Woe betide the retail CEO who does not have a strong argument to counter falling sales or reducing margins. Profit warnings are commonplace. Add to this the fact that the sector is sailing head-on into the storm that is the exponential growth of online purchasing while retaining a physical presence on the high street and retail parks, and you would be forgiven for thinking that it is simply a dog-eat-dog sector.

And yet many of the world's premier retailers have been around for decades, proving perhaps that there is something reassuringly enduring about the presence of a household name. Names like Walmart (United States), Metro (Germany), Tesco (UK), Costco (United States) and Aldi (Germany) are now to be found on every continent in some form or other, and they are all now faced with a conundrum – how to remain consistently profitable while retaining customer and brand loyalty, and being demonstrably mindful of the zeitgeist of responsibility to the planet and developing world – all in a business where the threat of substitution and capricious consumers is constant.

One might think that this is a difficult environment in which to model responsible leadership. Many retailers are acutely aware that to lead in their world is to have an advantage for a short time only. It is a world of fast copy and price warfare.

Marks & Spencer has embarked on a bold journey to become the world's most sustainable retailer. Fine words on paper, but what does this mean in practice and what has it to do with responsible leadership? More importantly, how can this goal be different from a simple CSR tick-box exercise?

To understand this bold goal, it is important to look back for a moment at the history of this company – widely regarded as one of the bellwether names on the UK (and increasingly global) retail high street.

The business had humble roots in the northern English city of Leeds, beginning in 1884 as a penny bazaar. As it grew, staying close to the community was important to its founders and by the 1930s the name Marks & Spencer was synonymous with trust, quality and, significantly, as an employer who looked after its employees, going beyond the minimum standards for wages, benefits and care. Such values set the business apart from other retailers and for the next 40 years or so the brand was unassailable. To work for Marks & Spencer was a job for life and a way of life.

As with many long-established businesses, there comes a time when other competitors copy and look for advantage in other areas. This was certainly the case for Marks & Spencer as other UK retailers assumed the leadership of the sector it once regarded as its own natural territory.

Faced with this diminishing of position, falling sales and a consumer base that was becoming increasingly fickle, the business set about trying to re-establish the brand as uppermost in the UK retail sector. Along with a rebrand of the logo (M&S was common parlance so it became the logo), together with necessary product reinvigoration and focus on key lines from time to time, one exciting aspect of this evolution has been a bold objective to differentiate itself from its competitors by leading the corporate debate around sustainability. Plan A.

The business had recognized that it had for too long dwelt on past glories when it was the employer of choice and known for quality above all else. Whether this was complacency or simply the natural life cycle of such an established business is not important. But according to Mike Barry, Director of Plan A, by the turn of the millennium M&S had lost its way and was registering less than 10 per cent on a sustainability scale.

The 1990s had seen the emergence of lobby groups targeting big retail brands about trading policies and this gave birth to the CSR responses that all serious corporates adopted. The emergence of the fair trade movement had been gathering steam for 10 years or more at this point. It had its roots in the 1970s with visionary people like Anita Roddick, who started The Body Shop with a mission to change the world's practices around testing cosmetics on animals and to source natural ingredients and promote fair trade. In many respects, her legacy has borne fruit and shaped much of the movement we know today.

M&S admits that it toed the line with CSR and in a moment of candour, Barry acknowledges that, for many years, along with the rest of the corporate world, it played a simple game of 'last one to tick the right box loses'. CSR had become nothing more than a box-ticking exercise largely involving saying the right things in the annual report. This is highlighted by Wayne Visser in his excellent book *The Age of Responsibility* (2011), in which he charts the evolution of CSR from greed through philanthropy to a bolder future of responsiveness that is in so many ways congruent with the messages in this book.

Then in 2000 the Finance Director, Alison Reid, took the courageous decision to employ a dedicated resource – Mike Barry – to drive the business towards a leadership position around sustainability. By 2006 Sir Stuart Rose, who had masterminded the turnaround of M&S, had called Barry into his office and told him that M&S was to be a leader in this area. It had won some awards but this was not enough for a business that was trying to pull away from its competitors through doing the right thing.

'Doing the right thing' is a phrase that occurs often in the CSR debate. For a time this was a differentiator for businesses, and indeed the ethical financial services crisis of 2008 highlighted that there were many different interpretations of 'the right thing', such that no one was actually doing it. Five years later, at the time of writing, it is my view that 'doing the right thing' has now become the price of entry to the game. But in 2006 it was something of a new phrase and phenomenon.

The strategy

Quite brilliantly, in 2007, the business came up with 'Plan A – because there is no Plan B' as its sustainability strategy (Marks & Spencer Group plc, 2007). The aim was to address the social and environmental impacts of the retail business and to draw customers' and employees' attention to policies and opportunities to support the business in fairer trading, positive impacts on climate change and the way the business uses natural resources and manages waste.

Barry acknowledges that, to begin with, this was essentially a functional plan that was for a while kept below the radar of public and city scrutiny. No fewer than

180 commitment objectives were set down to run alongside the business as usual objectives and measures. The areas of attention are:

- involve our customers in Plan A;
- make Plan A how we do business;
- climate change;
- waste;
- natural resources;
- fair partner;
- health and well-being.

Each year since 2007 these have been reported on openly, and in 2013 the business confidently stated that Plan A had achieved 139 of the commitments and delivered £135 million of net benefit to the bottom line.

According to Barry, Rose's successor as CEO, Marc Bolland, has laid down another challenge now, namely how to turn what has been a novel approach to sustainability into how normal business is done under a new strategic direction – How We Do Business. In essence, this aims to push beyond what has already been achieved and to find ways to bring the 80,000 staff, 2,000 suppliers and 35 million customers closer together in shaping the way the business is run.

The actions

Already, the business has started some imaginative schemes such as 'Shwopping', which has encouraged customers to bring unwanted clothing into the stores to be donated to Oxfam for reselling, recycling and reusing, thereby beginning to change mental models in the minds of customers. By linking the act of buying something new with the act of exchanging something old for it, M&S hopes to begin to change customers' habits and mindsets. According to Barry, this is important to the future of sustainable retailing, for example one in which all clothing garments are brought back for recycling before a new one is purchased.

This scheme is one example of M&S's approach to dip its toe in the water, to try things out, not aiming to do too much too quickly but to pace effort with customer and market expectations. Barry acknowledges that the vision is a long-term one that will require the company to hold its nerve and make smaller adjustments and initiatives. By linking small steps together, its leaders believe that they can create enough momentum to evolve the culture in the business. As a business that has traditionally tried to live by its core values, it believes that this is not a radical about-face, but more of a rediscovery and reconnection with its heritage.

The business has set itself the goal of ensuring that by 2020 every product in its range has a credible Plan A story behind it. This is no small undertaking as the retailer has thousands of products in its clothing, furnishings, household goods and food ranges. What this requires is an approach that brings the whole supply chain into an alignment around the values and practices embodied in Plan A. Communicating the mindset shift with suppliers becomes an important task.

M&S has acknowledged that this challenge is more than just a technical challenge. It is also a challenge of thinking among leaders, managers and staff. The company has invited all its top 100 senior leaders to undertake an immersion leadership development programme with a leading business school. This programme seeks to expose leaders to ethical dilemmas and other models of responsible leadership around the world, with the aim of helping them develop a strong understanding of their individual and collective moral compass.

The business has also partnered with other institutions in developing thought leadership around the sustainability agenda. In a recent study along with Accenture and BITC (Marks & Spencer and Accenture, 2013), they set out five areas for innovation:

- shared value bringing together wider interests of societies and communities;

- more with less by developing cleaner technologies and resource efficiency;

- circular economy improving recycling and creating circular business models;

- new consumption models enabling collaborative consumption and educating consumers;

- transparency and customer engagement by embedding sustainable supply chains and communicating openly with customers.

This form of leadership is congruent with the overall M&S approach of taking a leading position in the discussion. It is also beginning to challenge the definitions for success and attempting to quantify benefits of a new thinking. Furthermore, these innovations represent the core of responsible leadership in action, bringing stakeholders from around the system together to share the challenge and co-create the solution.

The learning

M&S admits that things will go wrong. It is, after all, a very big business and across 80,000 staff there is ample room for a bad decision here and there. Such is the nature of global businesses. However, by accepting that this is a journey of improvement and by not singing from the rooftops about getting it 100 per cent right at the outset it is managing expectations carefully. Barry stresses the importance of learning from each success and each mistake, so that the successes can become systemic and the mistakes do not become so. By having a key leader with a direct relationship with the board, there is clearly top-table support and sponsorship, seemingly in more than just words.

The company has been keen to point out that through successive CEOs the agenda is not changing significantly. This differs from other similar organizations that bring in new CEOs with a mandate to change things or turn things around. By playing to its strengths and connecting the future global sustainable narrative intentionally to the historical narrative of a community-focused employer, the embedding more deeply of Plan A within the culture is more likely.

Finally, M&S has challenged the paradigms around measuring success. It certainly measures sales and year-on-year performance, and has already been able to quantify its own progress on Plan A in terms of contribution to profit, but at the same time it is attempting to look beyond and see if it can define the future success for a retail business that touches so many parts of society. Again, the leadership of the business is approaching its role with a holistic purpose, seeing M&S as a key influence on the wider system. Whether it will succeed is the wrong question in many ways. It has begun on a path that will be very difficult to stop now. It has already succeeded in leading where many are now following.

Summary

During this chapter we have explored three dilemmas (among many) that present themselves to responsible leaders as they seek to thrive and make impact:

- Listening through the noise:
  - Recognize the effects of brain fatigue.
  - Acknowledge the illusion of busyness.
  - Listen deeply.
  - Cultivate serenity through focus.
- Looking for and seeing beyond the immediate:
  - Challenge assumptions.
  - Scan widely and dialogue effectively.
  - Value intuition.
  - Be intentional about ripples of influence and impact.

- Redefining success:
  - Challenge old mindsets and paradigms of growth and profit.
  - Embrace agility as a foundation for success.
  - Look for models of success in unusual places.
  - Consider 'how' and 'why' equally with 'what'.

Throughout Part 1 we have been exploring the case for responsible leaders and leadership. Without generating a precise formula and an exhaustive checklist, we have been able to offer some principles and some examples of what these principles look like in action. Our overriding sense is that to be a responsible leader is to be a leader who is at ease with his or her place in the system and is mindful of the impact that his or her actions have throughout it. He or she is someone who is at ease with paradox and uncertainty, having developed ways to thrive in our fast-paced and changing world; someone who embraces the revolution positively and seeks to 'add to' for the common good; someone who is more 'otherish' than 'selfish'.

In Part 2 we move on to consider how to develop leaders with such perspectives and how the organizations in which they work both help and hinder this.

PART TWO
The organizational response

Developing responsible leaders

> *The world we have created is a product of our thinking; it cannot be changed without changing our thinking.*
> **(ALBERT EINSTEIN)**

In Part 2, I will explore how organizations can focus on developing responsible leaders and a culture of responsibility. I accept that for some this may already be the reality as they have begun their journey, but for others this may be the starting point. To begin with, we will set out how leaders learn and how this informs development interventions. Appreciating that learning is more than 'going on a course' is important in the context of responsible leadership. I will use a case study from my own experience at PwC to illustrate this. We will then look more closely at one important approach to developing responsible leaders using experiential immersion opportunities. The ensuing chapters will examine how organizational culture shapes responses and what can be done by leaders to impact culture responsibly and mindful of the thinking from Part 1.

As before, I will encourage you to think about your own experiences and culture via some prompts for reflection and some practical suggestions.

CASE STUDY   PwC

Paul was a senior manager in PwC, the organization that I worked for as Head of Leadership and Talent. He was regarded by his superiors as talented and with potential for partnership. His career path was being carefully managed, exposing him to important roles on client assignments and within the business. One of his clients was a global telecommunications giant with a presence on every continent – a demanding client. The client had a difficulty in a territory in Africa and was seeking help from PwC. The difficulty was due to losing a key person in a key role in a key territory at a key time and without an obvious successor to hand. As a global business, it could have flown someone in to fill the gap, but instead chose to meet the immediate need by seconding an expert from PwC for a few months.

Working in Africa is typically both stimulating and frustrating at the same time. The challenges are complex and rewarding as economies are growing fast (from low bases) and advances in technology are bringing increases in consumerism against a backdrop of huge wealth inequality. The pervading organizational culture varies depending on the country and region, but as a generalization, leadership in business is demonstrated through positional power and force of will through a hierarchy. (This is often the picture of political leadership we see on our television screens and it is similar in many businesses.)

Paul was asked to take up this secondment position for a few months as he had been working on an assignment with the client and had built up a bank of trust and respect with it. Despite the fact that he had a young family, he chose to grasp the opportunity. His tenure of the interim role proved a great success, so much so that the company offered him the permanent role (which he declined). What had transpired was that Paul had approached the role very differently from others and from expectations. Rather than going in and mirroring the methods of predecessors, he did what he thought was the right way to lead, which was to listen, to understand and to involve in order to win commitment and build longer-term capability. As previously mentioned, this is quite unusual in Africa where leaders are expected to tell and direct. As a westerner he would have been quite free to do just that, as it was to be expected. But Paul realized that many of the problems were relational and behavioural, not structural.

One year previously, Paul had been with me and a larger team in Kenya participating in a leadership development programme with a difference. He was one of 50 emerging leaders from around the world invited to explore their world and their business through a number of challenging lenses with a view to broadening their understanding of what it might mean to lead effectively in the 21st century as part of a global business. A key message during the programme was that leaders not only needed to have a sense of direction and a vision with which to inspire people, but also personal humility to connect at a deeper level through understanding. When I interviewed Paul a while later, he said that it was the immersive experience in the slums of Nairobi and the discussions with Masai tribesmen that had shaped his leadership on this assignment. He realized that he did not know all the answers but that as an Englishman operating in West Africa he would be viewed through a particular lens based on people's previous experience. He knew then that he would have to behave differently from previous expat bosses if he was to win the support of the team and, more importantly, to have the team performing well in both the immediate and longer term. He chose to listen and involve, to get to know the people and understand their perspective on things. Paul made it to partner in the business and is back working in the UK for the time being.

Part 2 focuses on how organizations play a significant part in building or destroying a culture of responsibility. Given that we all work in systems, we all have opportunity to shape the system. But we must also be wise as to the system's influence on us as individual responsible leaders. As a colleague of mine says, it is how we remain in control of our part in the system and maintain our voice in it that shapes our leadership effectiveness.

This chapter sets out a case for thinking intentionally about developing responsible leaders. To begin with, it will be important to summarize what we know about how leaders learn and develop. Whereas this might be regarded by some as old ground and well understood, it is my view that there is still a lot of wasted time, money and effort across our field of leadership development through ignorance and distraction. I do not suppose that I have the complete answer but I will identify a series of questions based on comparing what we see in our work with researched examples of imaginative learning interventions.

My basic premise is that much of what is done under the banner of leadership development is only just beginning to address the need to develop *responsible* leaders, and in many cases is falling well short.

Enhanced learning cycle

Getting the balance between cognitive and emotional learning right

Learning theory identifies that as humans we learn through many different means. One of my children can learn from reading a textbook and taking past examination papers to pass examinations. He applies this knowledge to complex problems in the world of finance. Another of my children cannot learn that way. He can pass exams, but it is an ordeal requiring huge amounts of discipline and unnatural focus. He learns best through observing and then trying it out for himself. He is also a sports scientist who loves nothing more than applying insights to real people and their situations.

Honey and Mumford's work on learning styles (2006), based on the foundational work of David Kolb, helps us explore how people learn, as it identifies a cycle for learning starting with experiencing followed by reviewing, then concluding and finally planning. From this, Honey and Mumford identified that people will have a preference for learning based on these stages. Those who learn through doing (Activists) are drawn to experiences, those who learn through reflecting (Reflectors) prefer opportunities for reflection and review, those who learn through analysing and theorizing (Theorists) welcome the opportunity to see how things fit into the big picture and perhaps identify what else has been written on the subject, and finally those who learn by trying things out (Pragmatists) look to formulate their own ways forward and test them out. Honey and Mumford contest that we all learn from all aspects of the cycle but that we have a preferred approach, and that by the nature of preference, we will tend to gravitate to that at the expense of the others.

In my work with leaders I have found it helpful to amplify this. Figure 5.1 illustrates an enhanced learning cycle, and this is especially relevant as we seek to develop leaders who can respond to the challenges set out in Part 1 and who will pick up the baton for responsible leadership.

Learning happens when individuals connect what they are experiencing with their existing frames of thinking and emotions. If this reinforces positive emotional feelings, the experience usually reinforces existing patterns and they can proceed, repeating the same behaviour as it yields positive responses. If the situation changes, they may well try their usual behaviour until this is proven ineffective. If it proves ineffective, they are faced with a choice: to continue with a pattern or to adapt it or to learn, perhaps. If the situation is so new that it is outside their existing frames, they have a choice to be open to forming completely new frames or retreating into a safe place. **What is fundamental to learning is the responsibility on the individual to notice what is happening in the moment and to develop personal processes to evaluate the extent to which connections with normal patterns are happening.** Over time, as leaders get more experienced, this process can happen quickly and skilfully. If, however, the process takes a long time, individuals may find themselves in a state of extreme pressure and discomfort, which itself may yield learning (how do they deal with discomfort or indeed the discomfort faced by others around them). Worse still, individuals may deny that the

FIGURE 5.1   Enhanced learning cycle

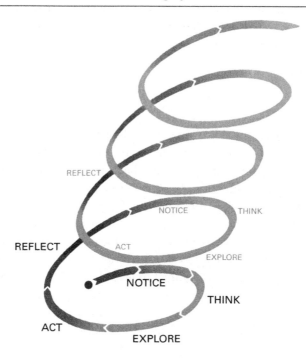

situation is any different and fail to notice that their normal patterns are proving unhelpful. They may succumb to a personal blind spot and fail to learn.

At this stage, I need to make a distinction between intellectual learning where a person is learning facts and information in order to repeat them or apply them to a theoretical assignment – the kind of learning that might typically be the norm at a school or university – and the learning that leaders need to do to be effective and responsible. As we have seen already in Part 1, countless senior leaders attended executive education programmes run by esteemed business schools the world over and yet the world still plunged into financial meltdown and we still have a crisis of trust in leadership. Developing responsible leaders is much more than analysing a case study and comparing it to a theoretical construct. Indeed, many top business schools are now reappraising their teaching approaches and increasingly moving away from a case approach to an experiential and 'real' approach. Some are embracing the need for more responsible leadership development for executives by providing MBAs focused on corporate and social responsibility or social enterprise. This is to be commended for many of the reasons we will touch on shortly.

Collectively we have realized that genuine leadership learning is both a cognitive *and* emotional process. It is also contextual for each person both based on the scenario in which the leader finds himself or herself and also dependent on his or her 'wiring' – values, goals, drives, preferences and capabilities.

Notice

To return to the expanded learning cycle, the first requirement is to notice. This requires being attentive and in a state of awareness. By way of an example, let us examine the scenario that introduced this chapter. The development programme that Paul experienced exposed him and his fellow participants to a very different set of experiences from their normal world. Distributing polio vaccines in the slums of Nairobi creates an emotional reaction. Discussing global and local agricultural policies and their impact on rural indigenous communities forces fresh thinking. The group of participants was encouraged to leave behind their normal models and be curious about what they were seeing, thinking and feeling. Using Gestalt techniques, they were invited to log and begin to process what they perceived as risky experiences and sensory observations – smells, sounds, heat, discomfort – in the security of an expertly facilitated dialogue. Such was the extreme difference from normal experience that it was easier for them to suspend their current reality (back in their corporate world) and throw themselves into the adventure. Yet they brought with them their human emotional responses such as shock, fear, disgust, shame and empathy. What became important was to help them individually notice and recognize their deeper responses alongside their logical and analytical assessments ('this is wrong'; 'we should fix this'). Paul and the group were asked to develop a mindset of being able to notice in the moment – to be attentive to what is happening around them first before jumping to a response.

Daniel Goleman in his well-known work on emotional intelligence (1996) calls on us to develop skills to read our own emotional state and to be socially aware, so that we can explore others' emotional responses with them. This requires skills of noticing. Practically, for example, during a business meeting we would encourage our clients to begin to notice (among other things):

- **Physical**: how am I reacting to the physical environment? How are others reacting to it? Is it helping or hindering?

- **Relational**: what do I notice about who is in the room and how they are relating to each other? How am I relating to people? Who is talking most/least? What is their impact on me and on others?

- **Contribution**: what is my contribution and how do I see it impacting the group and individuals? What are my emotional reactions to what is going on? What causes the strongest feeling for me (gut response)? To what extent am I (and others) being honest about our responses? How are others' emotions being demonstrated?

- **Process**: what body language is congruent and inconsistent? What words are people using? What tone am I detecting? How am I/are we responding to logical arguments and inspiring narratives, for example? How do people react to difficult moments?

In my experience, more often than not, these simple prompts are ignored in the least effective business meetings that we observe. Many coaching clients are shocked when they are encouraged simply to begin to notice, wondering how they have managed for so long without paying attention to this level of information. **To develop the skills and techniques of noticing is a critical leadership requirement as it orientates the leader to be open-minded and curious.** This in turn will facilitate generative discussions rather than close down early. Noticing is about paying attention to the physical, logical, emotional (perhaps even spiritual or soulful) insights and reactions both for oneself and for others in the scenario.

Think

What was important for Paul and his colleagues was to provide the space and forum for surfacing the questions that they had, based on what they were noticing. Feelings of shock or shame generate powerful reactions. But to respond in a knee-jerk way is not often the most mature and effective. Basic neuroscience tells us that such negative emotions cause defensive or aggressive behaviours at worst, or at best ill-judged responses. For example, giving $100 to a poor family in a Nairobi slum may well be a knee-jerk immediate response to noticing injustice or shame (I should be doing something about this – I can do something as I have money), but it does not change anything for the better. If anything, it makes things worse as the family is suddenly the focus of unwanted attention, and as they have no way of sustaining wealth.

First and foremost, to be a responsible leader is to take full responsibility for one's contribution and to use personal leadership as a force for good in a situation or leadership moment. Therefore, responsible leaders recognize that there are questions and hypotheses in all these leadership moments. They spend time naming these for themselves internally. A process that we encourage people to follow might include:

- **Natural reactions:** Based on what I notice, what is my most natural or default response? How might this land in this moment?

- **Assumptions:** What assumptions am I making about this situation and my role in it? How am I balancing emotion with logic/reason? What other theories might I (or others) generate about this moment?

- **Goals:** What am I trying to achieve here, and why? How can I add to this situation positively?

- **Players:** Who else is/could be/should be involved? Who should not be involved? Who has power, and why? How do they exercise it?

- **Time:** What time frame am I working on – immediate vs longer term, for example?

During the development programme, the emerging leaders were encouraged to name the assumptions they were making and would therefore be basing their actions upon. One such assumption, for example, is that well-being is a function of material wealth. Walking through the slums of Nairobi is not comfortable, but it is uplifting as much as it is depressing. The capacity for human beings to be creative in the face of suffering is huge. Tiny plots of land can be cultivated. Small retail booths proliferate. People do things for each other. Communities gather around cafés, churches, schools, TVs, all located in tin shacks or rudimentary buildings. Clearly there are negative forces at work too. Drugs and drink are an easy and quick way out of suffering. Tribal heritage plays an important role in the nation (as it does in so many nations of the world), and these boil over during elections or power struggles. Responsible leaders ask questions about power, where it lies and how it is used.

Thinking is about:

- surfacing (tough) genuine questions that noticing begins to raise;

- naming assumptions that are present, helpfully or unhelpfully;

- beginning to form some hypotheses that can be tested and discussed.

Explore

Given that modern responsible leaders have a systemic mindset and world-view, key evidence of this is their ability to learn through exploration either on their own or with others. What we mean by exploration is tackling the questions and assumptions from the previous stage through dialogue and discussion.

Returning to the development programme in Kenya, for Paul to learn from his experiences he needed to make sense of the emotions, challenge his assumptions and then explore what this might mean for him personally (and the group). In our view, this process of exploration involves listening at a number of levels.

First, listening to your own voice and what might be happening deeper in your own inner self and soul. For Paul, this might have involved recognizing that he felt anger at injustice and that although he realized that he could not do anything significant immediately, he could nonetheless acknowledge his desire to do something and take up some personal responsibility. He might have envisioned himself visiting Kenya again or sponsoring an enterprise or an individual in the country. His inner voice might have been challenging him to restore some balance in his life back in his real world. He was generating choices. This is important for responsible leaders.

Secondly, inviting contributions and insight from others and listening through genuine dialogue might have helped Paul to generate further choices for moving forward himself and also help the group move forward collectively.

As facilitators, in order to develop genuine dialogue in a leadership development context, we encouraged the group to practise the skills of suspending immediate judgements about suggestions and to recognize intent in the ideas coming from self and others. This ability does not come easily as we are programmed to evaluate quickly, and in the task-based cultures that exist in many organizations, opinions count. What is important for responsible leaders is to hold on to the possibility that something more might emerge from respectful dialogue. Perhaps something surprising or something that was not present within the individuals, but when they come together it emerges as a way forward or an option to consider. Such a willingness to create the space for generative dialogue is a mark of a receptive culture and one that is likely to embrace new ideas and paradigms.

This is more than creative brainstorming. It is grappling with tough issues intentionally and carefully. It may involve silence and deep pondering. It may involve meditating for a while on a key phrase or conundrum until some insight comes. I appreciate that this may sound like a long process, and developing responsible leaders can indeed be a long process as they become accustomed to the practices of stilling their quick thinking. Mindfulness techniques are helpful as they slow down our crowded minds and allow insights to emerge from our subconscious. I do not intend to go into these in detail, but there are many good guides for these practices available. However, it is worth noting that the practice of retreating for a defined period of time is proven to stimulate rest and re-creation and, from that, insight. How many of us get the answers to some of our deepest issues and problems when we are on holiday?

For Paul and his group of emerging leaders, the exploration was facilitated through a time spent in the bush, camping without the trimmings of normal life (no phones, no e-mails, limited comforts). Three days and nights under the open skies of the Mara surrounded by wild animals and guarded by tall Masai with spears proved to be an incubator for great conversation and listening. It was also an opportunity to observe and learn from completely different cultures, in this case the Masai tribespeople.

How then can this stage be transferred into the normal world? At one end of a continuum, we encourage leaders to find times to pause and retreat. This is typically for one day and often involves walking and talking with a coach or facilitator. It can be for longer and, indeed, can be just as effective for a couple of hours, say, over a lunchtime concert in a city-centre venue.

Such practices are not possible, though, during a crowded meeting agenda. And yet, once someone has cultivated the habit of slowing down their thinking and listening better, they can invite different contributions from members. They can easily name assumptions and, in so doing, invite others to explore before jumping to conclusions. Nancy Kline, in her work *Time to Think* (1999), provides invaluable guidelines for leaders and participants in meetings. I want to highlight two of her ten principles (they are all indispensable) that help develop patterns that in turn facilitate better learning. First, the principle of giving everyone a defined turn (within a time frame) and valuing each contribution. As Kline says: 'Knowing they won't be interrupted frees people to think faster and say less.' This is critical to good dialogue. Secondly, inviting diverse contributions. Kline adds: 'Diversity raises the intelligence of groups. Homogeneity is a form of denial.' This is certainly important to avoid the phenomenon of 'group think' where no one is prepared to step out of line. Furthermore, to be globally responsible leaders requires seeing different perspectives.

In our experience, simple practices to enhance exploration genuinely facilitate learning and better outcomes. Moreover, they do not take up lots of time. They require discipline and intentionality:

- Label the step of exploration openly so everyone is on board.
- If it is a step to be done on your own, make it clear in your mind what you are doing and create breathing space (this can be done

even during a meeting with a well-timed comfort break, for example).

- Listen to your inner voice individually.
- Foster a climate of good listening for everyone – often slowing things down.
- Value silence.
- Agree on and name assumptions and hold them openly.
- Suspend judgements about contributions.
- Invite and encourage insights – look for emerging insights that were not present beforehand.
- Be comfortable with choices as a result of the exploration stage.

Act

Learning is only learning if it is applied. The earlier stages of this approach encourage the learner to focus his or her attention and to develop practices that generate insights. When exploration is done, the learner needs to apply insights in his or her context and to make sense of how effective this is. As we develop responsible leaders, this often involves stepping up to the plate and taking a stand or making something happen in a leadership moment – **role-modelling a new or different behaviour**, for example.

When faced with the challenges of getting people to buy into new processes in the finance function in an African office of a global telecoms giant, Paul was faced with a choice to repeat the behaviours that had been employed thus far or to role-model what he believed would be more likely to succeed. But rather than simply do what he would be inclined to do in his normal western context, he was wise enough to modify his approach and include his understanding of African cultural nuances. Mindful that status is important to African males, he was astute enough not to undermine this. Mindful also that women in that part of Africa often carry the weight of work and responsibility, he was also aware that he needed to win their support quickly and give them sufficient empowerment to win their trust. Most likely not everything would go smoothly, so being comfortable **testing things out and prototyping** his ideas about roles and structure meant that he would have to adapt. He sought to **co-create** with his team the future for their function without him in the role. For responsible leaders who step outside the normal and accepted parameters, there can be personal risk alongside the organizational risk of things not working out. And what we know about learning and leadership is that the more skilled a person is in the first three stages of the cycle (noticing; thinking; exploring), the more he or she can minimize these risks.

In Part 1, we mentioned the peace process in Northern Ireland and the degree of reconciliation between the nationalists and unionists. The earlier stages of the cycle took decades of pain and suffering until key leaders spent long enough in the exploring phase to challenge their assumptions and work out where they were more similar than different. Only then could role-modelling of a brave new way gain traction. Importantly for that part of the world, it was the act of co-creating the future that galvanized people, rather than one side taking the credit. Sadly, the learning process cost many lives over the years, from the 1960s to the 2000s.

During the experiential leadership programme we have been following, we were able to provide the participants with the opportunity to plan for applying their learning back in the normal world. These plans ranged from some participants who intended to approach their clients and start a real dialogue around sustainable and ethical business practices, where they felt that there was a genuine need or that they might get a warm reception, through to one young Russian woman who wanted to tackle the issue of excessive workloads in her office in Moscow. Her intention was not to limit the workloads, as the market was demanding the response of the business, but to think creatively and plan to discuss the establishing of a crèche for young mothers to have their children close by during working hours. In her view, a view shared by other leaders on the programme, the issue was how to adapt to the reality and also to attract skilled young mothers back to work by removing the emotional stress of having a young infant miles (and hours) away. She had noticed her emotional reactions with her own child, and the process of seeing working mothers in Kenya with their children by their side or provided for nearby had stimulated in her the ideas for replicating this in Moscow. To implement this would require the winning of support from senior leaders, but she was willing to try.

In summary, the Act stage involves:

- being prepared to role-model different or new ideas;
- being open to test out and prototype new ideas;
- actively seeking to co-create with others to cement buy-in and ownership;
- accepting personal and collective risk by stepping forward to lead in the moment and context.

Reflect

Finally, to complete this expanded learning cycle, we know that leaders who learn deeply return to the reflection process through pausing to review. Far too frequently, leaders confront problems with the mindset that there is a quick solution to be found, which leads to a paradigm of rapid response – 'something must be done, this is something, therefore we can try this'; for example, this team is not working, we need a team away-day, this is the kind of thing that we have done in the past, therefore we can do it like this again. It sounds far fetched, but we encounter this with worrying regularity when we are approached by our clients. This is amateur thinking and is not going to bring about the changes in culture that some organizations and businesses need to effect if they are to be allowed to play in the brave new game where responsibility is a differentiator. It is as if some organizations are stuck in the trap of thinking of an option and simply acting quickly in an expensive cycle of ineffective learning.

A financial services client of mine was confronted by some disappointing employee feedback that suggested that leadership and management were not inspiring top performance and that the turnover rates among some grades were unacceptable. Despite much discussion, they were convinced that a one-day leadership essentials programme would bring about changes in behaviour. In the fast-moving financial services world, it was deemed unacceptable for people to be away from their desks for longer than a day (quite what happened during holidays or sickness is another matter), and so a traditional workshop/course would be required. A compromise was reached that involved participants being asked to prepare for half a day beforehand and to focus on real scenarios in their specific teams, while then planning to apply and review a very few salient learning points over four weeks after the workshop. Their full attendance and attention on the workshop was required. Unfortunately, despite the workshop itself presenting people with uncomfortable challenges and some real insights, the programme had limited impact because the culture in the business did not embrace the full learning cycle and paid little attention to reflection and review and to the practices that make this stage in the cycle so valuable. Preparation work was not done consistently, questionnaires were not delivered to the right places, reviews with line managers did not happen, coaching support was patchy at best. Regrettably, the culture in that part of the organization was that learning happened on a course alone and that simple attendance equated to learning.

This simple yet painful episode illustrates the importance of organizational responsibility for supporting learning, and for individual leaders, the value of this reflection stage. Leaders are busy people. The pressures of short-term performance and the immediacy of operational challenges draw attention, energy and focus. It is hard to resist. I have lost count of the number of managers and delegates I have coached who tell me that despite planning to spend time planning and strategizing, they have been sucked back into a culture of back-to-back meetings with no time to review progress or even take stock. We must not underestimate the likelihood of this stage being the one that is skimped. And yet, for behaviour to change and learning to happen, it is essential. Kolb, Honey and Mumford proved this. We have tried to amplify it further in our work.

This stage of the cycle again requires leadership attention, a recurring theme throughout – where attention and focus are given, learning happens. Planning to review meetings, for example, seems to most to be a no-brainer and yet leaders run from meeting to meeting simply accumulating tasks and to-do lists. Kline notes that it is important to build review moments into actual meetings (and training workshops) so that people develop the habit. Cultivating the habit of capturing insights and personal learning in the moment and then reviewing them, say at the end of the day or week, helps leaders make sense of their fast-moving world.

The reflect stage is about asking challenging questions of self and others. For example: To what extent have I been focused on applying the learning? Have I given it my best shot? What traps have I fallen back into that have prevented me from learning? What has surprised me about how I've been able to put things into practice? Such an **honest appraisal can yield real insight and naturally flows to greater noticing** (stage one of the cycle).

We know that seeking feedback is an important development process. Asking the tough questions of others about personal performance or application of learning, and embracing fully the responses, is a trademark of responsible leaders. It is common practice to invite learners to undertake a 360° or equivalent process before a development intervention, as a benchmarking step, and embracing these principles throughout the learning cycle can really help ground the learning.

Beyond the 'so what' test

A further point to note here is that **learning is the responsibility of the learner.** This may sound trite, but it is a key differentiator for responsible leaders – they take personal responsibility for their actions *and* their learning.

What this means in practice is that they are positively looking for connections between events, leadership moments and insights. They use the enhanced learning cycle to move beyond the 'so what' test. By way of example, a client of mine said during a planning session for a workshop that people would want the workshop to have some real 'takeaways', otherwise they would be inclined to say that it was all very nice but 'so what?' Again, this is amateur and irresponsible thinking based on a paradigm around learning that is stuck in the dark ages, namely that the job of the trainer is to present information and the role of the learner is to critique this and decide whether it is worth taking on board. Such an approach is linked to a 'busyness' mindset and compartmentalized approach. A participant's mental process might follow thus:

> I am a busy man. I have given up time for this workshop so it better be worthwhile. I will have to evaluate whether it's any good. We had better get some action points from this session that we can take away. I want the trainer to give me something useful. I have a busy day tomorrow so the clearer these are the better.

It sounds as if I have made this up, and yet I have heard this many times in one form or another. Its roots are in a mindset that is based on work (perhaps even life) being a series of meetings and separate events that are not integrated or interdependent. In this kind of world, people move from one event to another, accumulating action points but failing to see if there are any connections between them, or that learning can be in the spaces between or in the process of wrestling with some apparent tensions and conflicts. This requires the systemic approach we have been highlighting. It takes learning to a deeper place that is built on personal accountability. Rather than critique as the default process, responsible leaders look for surprises in the stretch zone beyond their personal comfort zone. Rather than immediate actions, they are happy with the possibility of ambiguity and emergent connections while also being alert to the obvious and immediate. Their 'so what' test might follow thus:

> I am a busy man. This opportunity has come at a difficult time but nonetheless it is an opportunity that may give me some interesting insights for my role. I need to remain open to noticing and exploring rather than closing things down. I might be surprised by myself or others. I'm accountable for gleaning value from this time and I'm optimistic that I can make it time well spent by listening well and contributing from my experience and my world.

This kind of mindset is reinforced by conversations between line managers and learners that emphasize accountability both before and after, and throughout the year. Reminding people of their commitments to apply learning over time embeds it in their normal world.

Clearly, if the learning intervention is poorly constructed or facilitated, there is a responsibility to say so constructively and, in my experience, when this is done from a generous and contributory stance, there is mutual benefit and the intervention can itself be evolved.

A word about **coaching and support**. We will return to this later, but for now I want to highlight that as humans we tend to value the external sounding board that helps us make sense of our learning, be it a teacher in first grade or a university professor, a scout leader or soccer coach, an executive coach or business mentor. Since the dawn of history, we have sought counsel because we intuitively recognize the benefit of talking something through and learning from others.

Leadership can be a lonely place. It is not uncommon for senior leaders to report that as they have acquired leadership positions, the nature of their relationships has changed. The adage that people only tell leaders what they think they want to hear is not without substance. Our earlier examples of poor judgements in Part 1 could in part be attributed to board discussions or executive discussions that were potentially inadequate, allowing a forceful, charismatic leader to get his or her own way without sufficient challenge or learning. Given that leadership is a full-on role and people in the organization feel that they have a right to a piece of the leader's energy or time, it is critically important for leaders to make space for reflection that enables them to complete the learning cycle. Supported by an experienced coach or mentor, this process can become invaluable.

One scenario that we have seen to be highly important is the use of coaching to support the transition process to a new role as a leader seeks to navigate the new relationships and make his or her mark in the new role. The commonly held view that the first 100 days is critical is accurate, although in our experience this period can be longer, more likely closer to six months.

For programmes that focus on developing responsible leaders, the coaching support can be even more important, which we will discuss next.

In summary, however, the Reflect stage involves:

- focusing attention once again on learning alongside tasks – making time and space to review;
- asking tough questions of oneself and forming an honest appraisal of progress;
- seeking and embracing feedback;
- enlisting coaching support to help process learning.

The habit of learning

The enhanced learning cycle has one additional dimension to emphasize. The cadre of responsible leaders we discussed in Part 1 is aware of the need to advance in their learning towards new experiences or to a deeper (or more advanced) level. They have recognized that to stand still in the modern world is to go backwards and lose relevance. They are also not content to repeat things just for the sake of it, expecting different results each time. They become skilled and comfortable with the processes we have highlighted in the cycle. They move quickly around the cycle, learning from as many occasions as they can. They appreciate that learning happens every day while they are working in their role and from surprising sources outside their workplace. Time spent with leaders with this orientation is often characterized by stimulating sessions that can also be personally challenging. **For as they learn, responsible leaders are committed to facilitating this kind of learning in others around them.** They cultivate the habit of learning. They do not allow their people to settle, encouraging them to push boundaries and explore how they can impact the system positively. I can think of many of my clients who started out as driven individuals focusing exclusively on tasks but have developed their motivations to embrace developing others and shaping the culture of the organization around them. This is a mark of responsible leaders – they progress things and learn throughout.

Reflections

- As you think about your own personal approach to learning, how skilled are you at recognizing learning opportunities and moving around the enhanced learning cycle intentionally?

- In which aspects of the cycle are you most comfortable and which least so? Why is this?

- In your organization, how does learning mostly happen? To what extent are there different emphases that could be used to help people learn?

- To what extent is your organization a place that develops responsible leaders and holds individuals accountable for their personal learning and progress?

Creating impactful and lasting development opportunities

Rather than provide a comprehensive list of development methods, I want to highlight one specific approach that can accelerate learning and is especially important in addressing the need for responsible leadership development. This approach, however, does come with a significant downside.

The leadership development programme that was run by PwC for emerging leaders in Kenya is an example of an **immersion programme**, one in which learning is framed within a very different experience from the participant's normal world.

Historically, this might have been limited to an outdoor-learning programme that involved physical team-building activities or problem-solving. Such programmes have their place and continue to be used to develop leaders the world over. The exaggerated and concentrated moments as a team is struggling to complete a task and wrestling with the dynamics within the team are powerful learning moments. Participants are facilitated to move round the enhanced learning cycle and make sense of feedback as they build a picture of their own personal leadership. However, such programmes typically do not go far enough to develop responsible leaders who are the embodiment of the people we talked about in Part 1 – those who can see beyond the immediate and impact the wider system.

A new genre of development opportunity is now emerging and in our experience it contains the following elements:

- **contracting** – working closely with the 'on the ground' experiences to clarify roles and how learning will take place;

- **orientation** – to create awareness and foundational skills to prepare the individuals and groups for the immersion;

- **immersion** – the learning experience itself;

- **support** – ongoing support during the immersion phase;

- **re-entry** – an intentional and managed process to enable smooth return to the 'normal world';

- **ongoing dialogue and support** – to enable sense-making and transfer of learning over significant time.

Contracting

To set up an impactful and well-run immersion experience requires on-the-ground support – literally in some cases. Many organizations will not have this expertise, particularly if the experience is to happen overseas. However, it is important not to skimp on this stage, and so it can be valuable to enlist the help of a brokering organization or non-governmental organization (NGO) or similar that understands the full reality on the ground. Typically, for a responsible leadership development programme the immersion will be in an organization that operates in a completely different sector. For us at PwC, this meant working in the UK in the third sector, where not-for-profits and social enterprises face huge challenges of skilling themselves up, finding resources, developing marketing plans, influencing stakeholders, and managing finances and performance. Many of these challenges were the same for overseas organizations.

An important point, however, is that not all immersion programmes need to happen in charities or not-for-profits. Increasingly, businesses are using secondments into other businesses or sectors to provide a challenging and stimulating immersion experience. Such secondments can be for, ideally, a minimum of one month up to a maximum period of 12 months. After that, in reality it ceases to be a secondment and becomes more of a placement.

Questions to be addressed in this contracting phase include:

- What is the scope of the immersion experience?
- Is the learner/are the learners there to carry out tasks, provide support, give advice, coach internal people, or observe and listen?
- For how long is this going to last?
- How can we ensure that the immersion does not become a disruption to the receiving organization?
- Who are the key people to engage with and how best to do this?
- What can the receiving organization expect and not expect from the immersion learning? What is the added value to both parties?
- What is realistic by way of time commitment?
- Is there any fee to change hands?
- Who on the ground is responsible for ensuring the smooth running of the immersion experience?
- How will contact be maintained throughout?

- How can the receiving organization be involved in the orientation phase and the application and reviewing phases?
- What is the likely ongoing commitment from both parties? (It is not uncommon, for example, for a secondee to continue to offer support or join a trustee board.)

Orientation

Ensuring that leaders are ready for an immersion experience is critical to learning effectiveness. Earlier, we examined the enhanced learning cycle and it is important for leaders to be exposed to this thinking and encouraged to experiment with it ahead of the intensity of an immersion experience. For example, during the Responsible Leadership Programme at PwC, participants were invited to learn mindfulness techniques and advanced listening skills along with some early examples of dialogue, so that they could move quickly to and through these stages in practice. Learning how to recognize insights when they occur will be invaluable during the intensity of a very different experience.

As we have seen thus far, the extent to which potential participants have a clear sense of their personal core is critical. An experienced coach should be allocated to spend time with each person to work on the elements of this that we discussed in Part 1. This will also provide the opportunity to discuss how the learner is going to manage the time away from his or her normal world both at work ('Who is going to man the fort while I am away?' How do we stop everything falling apart when I am not here?') and at home ('How do my family cope if I am away for several weeks?'). Someone with a solid core and foundation is more likely to be able to cope well with this than someone for whom these insights are still forming.

Then potential participants can be exposed to the responsible leadership systems framework that will allow them to begin to formulate their own hypotheses ahead of time. These can then be the starting point for the experience and they can begin to frame some of their questions and approaches.

Using the model, potential participants can begin to consider how this kind of thinking can and should apply to their business. This will help the later transfer of insights. Next, the receiving organization can be connected with the learner informally, so that they can begin to craft how the immersion experience will work in practice. Finally, we have found that potential participants should be required to craft their own rationale for attending, how this fits with their personal leadership/life journey and how they have brought on board support from a key business sponsor. In a nutshell, this orientation stage can be the make or break point for the innovative learning programme.

Immersion

I want to highlight some different immersion experiences that I have used and come across to help us identify how they work in practice.

At one end of the continuum for immersion is the kind of experience that select leaders are now beginning to take, in which they might spend up to six months working for an NGO in a developing country, offering advice and guidance while learning about a very different world. (VSO – Voluntary Services Overseas – provides opportunities for people to spend one or two years working overseas and although these technically are immersion experiences, they are more life changes for a season than organizationally relevant learning opportunities.) PwC uses this route for some global leaders, allocating them to projects in places such as Mexico, East Timor or South Africa, working on AIDS projects, community health projects, recycling rubbish or developing a business model for a sustainable business. Such projects can require the individual to break from his or her family and workplace and can be stressful, so it is important to be fully aware of this and put in place practical steps to mitigate the impact.

Less extreme but equally intense might be a shorter immersion experience in the home country, working in a different sector or with a social enterprise, which is also used at PwC. The same principles apply, but the time away from the workplace and family can be limited to, say, three to four weeks. From our experience, this approach lends itself better to learning transfer, which we will come to shortly.

Another approach, rather than requiring a once-only period of immersion time, encourages participants to spend many different moments of contact over an extended period of time. This can be with one organization, but it also works well when it is structured around a variety of immersion experiences. One company I know that does this especially well is Common Purpose, a social enterprise founded by Julia Middleton that specializes in developing leaders around the world. Julia is a modern-day responsible leader and is determined to develop leaders for the future who are also systemic in their perspective. She champions the principle of co-creation through the development programmes that Common Purpose provides. The key modus operandi for Common Purpose is to bring together players from different facets of society (public bodies, politicians, business leaders, religious leaders, communities and so on) and have them explore and dissect a city's or region's issues with the aim of generating new ideas and solutions based on shared understanding. Its approach cherishes diversity of perspective and recognizes that many solutions for tomorrow's problems will only emerge when relevant protagonists come together to co-create them. In her insightful book *Beyond Authority* (2007) she provides a strong case for how individuals can develop their leadership outside the boundaries of formal positional power for the greater good. (Emerging responsible leaders would be well advised to include this on their reading list.) These immersion experiences have the key advantage of allowing participants to continue to operate in their 'normal world' while at the same time experiencing visits to the 'different worlds' in their city or region to listen, question, discuss and explore.

Finally, I have come across mini immersion experiences that are one step removed from the token CSR 'let's paint a classroom' intervention. The small centre for outdoor learning that we met in Part 1 has developed a strong relationship with a large corporate financial services business, which invites members of the business to visit the centre over several occasions to develop a relationship with it and the team there. They can then add value through practical support while also gaining a deeper understanding of the 'different world' and learn about their own personal responses to some of the ongoing challenges.

Looking for creative ways to provide immersion experiences that are meaningful is beginning to set forward-thinking and responsible organizations apart from the crowd. Moreover, having such a development programme on a resumé speaks of depth and a long-term perspective.

Support

A word about **support during the immersion phase. Organizations that get this right stay close to any leaders who are away on a development opportunity.** For longer and intense experiences I have seen this done well through weekly calls or video sessions with a learning specialist to coach the participant around the learning cycle. I have myself been alongside participants during some of the occasions and used the immediacy to coach sense-making in the moment through journalling (capturing immediate thoughts and reactions, for example in a notebook). Whatever the approach taken, participants typically greatly value the expert ear and voice during what can be intense and uncomfortable learning experiences. Poorly managed assignments can leave participants feeling detached and divorced from the business and their people. This can exacerbate feelings of discomfort.

Re-entry

Earlier, I mentioned that this powerful learning method had several advantages, but one significant challenge for the organization. This is typically around re-entry and ongoing support.

Picture the scene – you have been away for one month working with an NGO in a developing region and you have discovered a depth in yourself that you previously had not encountered. Moreover, you have thought through how your current organization is performing against your new-found responsible leadership indices. You have done your best to stay in contact throughout the assignment and your learning has been profound on many levels. Your first day back to your normal routine is a Monday and you have to attend a regular monthly management meeting. Your mind is elsewhere and you find it difficult to give the meeting your full attention. Your team politely enquires about your leadership course and you share your experiences over a lunchtime session. While away, you devised some plans and ideas for how your organization could change to reflect the new order. You meet the CEO, who shows interest, but you detect that this is a gesture rather than a genuine openness to explore and change. He has not been on the programme and although he sponsored the opportunity, his language is focused more on what this will mean to your personal and departmental performance. Over the coming months, you are able to outwork some of your goals around becoming more responsible as a leader: locally, in your team, through supporting members in external opportunities, and for yourself by staying close to the not-for-profit you spent some time with during the immersion experience. Regrettably, you feel that it has been too hard to influence some of the hardliners in the management team and inspire them to think more long-term and look for different measures of success.

This may sound extreme, but it is all too common when we work with individuals and organizations around culture change and responsible leadership. For development professionals, it is imperative that we are cognizant of difficulties around re-entry. It is unprofessional to expose people to a powerful learning experience that impacts their heart and soul, to encourage them to think big and to aspire to change patterns in their normal world, only to send them back unprepared to influence key stakeholders in their normal system.

We have found that a re-entry workshop immediately following the immersion experience is an important step. This will provide a safe space for participants to come together and share their stories without the pressures of having to justify themselves to others who did not participate. This kind of workshop can be creative, using **storytelling** (helping participants use a variety of narrative techniques to communicate passionately and rationally), **art** (using professional artist facilitators), **audio-visual elements** (perhaps making a video), or **theatre and real players** (to enact likely scenarios where a participant might be required to influence a sceptic, for example).

It can also include one-to-one coaching to help the participants make sense of their learning in the context of their workplace and the realities therein; for example, identifying the stakeholders who will be curious and possibly supportive; those who will be passionately interested and keen to back any new learning; those cynics and sceptics who will want to expose this kind of development as a waste of time and money; those ambivalent people who will simply remind participants that the real world is all about short-term performance and meeting targets. Once these have been identified, strategies can be formulated to influence them or enlist their support. What is clear, however, is that a good understanding of organizational culture and systems thinking will go some way to preventing wasted effort and disillusionment. Acknowledging that short-term performance is the default mindset and that this is fundamentally not deliberately obstructive liberates returning participants to think carefully and responsibly about how to bring their narrative to life so that it paces the culture rather than comes at it at such a tangent that it bounces off 'back into orbit'. In the next chapter we will explore how to work with some organizational cultural forces for change.

Ongoing dialogue and support

Already in this book we have met some senior leaders who both get the imperative for leadership to be more responsible and model it with their actions. Richard Oldfield and Ian Powell at PwC, Marc Bolland at M&S, Paul Polman at Unilever and Steve Chalke at Oasis are working hard to align their organizational and personal values and to support others in their businesses on the journey. Unfortunately, in large organizations there are many levels of leadership that may not imbibe the narrative, for whatever reason. This could be genuine ideological opposition ('I don't believe this stuff – it's nonsense'), political opposition ('It was not invented here so we will stifle it', 'This up-and-coming leader is getting more air time than me so I will trash the ideas'), performance opposition ('This is all very good but we have some real priorities to focus on now – targets to hit – and this is a distraction') or traditional resistance ('This is a fad that will fade in time so we will carry on as if nothing has happened; what we do at the moment seems to work well enough').

It is therefore important for senior leaders to continue active sponsorship and dialogue with participants from impactful learning programmes to reassure them that the experience and learning have clear value to the business. Formal mentoring programmes facilitate such insights. This should be done in partnership with both organizational development and learning and development professionals who are fully bought in – ideally having themselves been through the learning experiences.

Aspirant responsible leaders should also be encouraged, where practical and appropriate, to continue relationships with their receiving organizations to model the long-term and relational approach embodied in responsible leadership thinking. Where they can continue with a team or action-learning group, this is valuable. Common Purpose, for example, creates extensive alumni networks in and across territories to help embed learning.

An important way to cement learning is to pass it on. Where it may not be possible for large numbers of people to attend long immersion experiences, it may be feasible for a team or department to create its own version locally and on a smaller scale. Once the principles are understood, a skilled responsible leader can facilitate movement around the enhanced learning cycle for his or her managers. Lots of people co-creating a different future on a local scale is how large-scale transformation takes place across an organization.

Finally, emergent responsible leaders can be encouraged to find opportunities to speak about and share their experience outside the organization. Writing articles, blogs, speaking at conferences and mentoring in another organization or community all reinforce messages at a deeper level for a participant. And as they develop personal 'responsible habits and patterns' that are different, their language evolves. What they regard as important changes. Their definitions of success become more imaginative.

Reflections

- How is learning valued and championed in your organization?

- How are people encouraged to take personal responsibility for their learning and work through the stages of a more advanced learning cycle?

- What approaches do you use in your organization to help emerging leaders develop a more responsible and systemic perspective?

- How can you be more imaginative and creative as you think about learning and development opportunities for yourself, your team and your organization?

- How, if appropriate, could you use aspects of learning through immersion experiences both personally and organizationally?

- What challenges would this kind of approach present for you, your team and your organization?

Summary

- During this chapter we have focused on how leaders learn deeply through an enhanced learning cycle of: noticing – thinking – exploring – acting – reflecting.

- We have begun to appreciate that by focusing on the learning processes we can develop habits and patterns so that they become our default; we can transfer these to our everyday workplaces and become skilful in noticing in the moment or generating questions that challenge assumptions.

- Using these insights we can build development opportunities for aspiring responsible leaders that are more impactful than purely classroom-based interventions.

- One such type of programme involves a period of immersion in a 'different world' that allows participants to have a depth and range of experience that accelerates personal learning. Such immersion is often based in an organization or place that challenges perceptions about leadership and responsible leadership specifically. They require careful planning and managing to be effective.

- Whereas these immersion opportunities enable powerful learning when handled well, we also recognize that organizations can be unintentionally complicit in dampening enthusiasm and frustrating participants. Careful thought is needed to facilitate effective re-entry and ongoing support.

Having considered how leaders learn and can be developed, the good work done through such programmes can so easily be undone by the practices and structures that comprise an organization's overarching culture. Attending to this is a crucial act of leadership and in the next chapter we will look more closely at how organizations can evolve a culture that both embeds learning and promotes responsible leadership.

Evolving a culture of responsible leadership

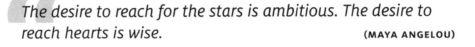

06

The desire to reach for the stars is ambitious. The desire to reach hearts is wise. **(MAYA ANGELOU)**

During this chapter we will explore the difference between a culture that is rooted in responsibility and one that is focused on compliance, in order to draw some comparisons and identify what this means for the responsible leader. We will then look at some practical ways to evolve a culture where more responsibility is evident across the organization. I say evolve as I believe that the term 'culture change' is now so widely used that it has become derided. Moreover, evolution respects aspects of a culture that are strong and laudable while also allowing for progress towards something that could be better. As before, we will offer some questions for your personal reflection as you build your own picture of your and other organizations.

A widely held and simple definition of culture is 'the way things are done around here; the way we do things'. Within this simple definition the implication is that culture is about actions, behaviours and choices. It is observable and by analysing incidents and patterns we can deduce what is actually done, which in theory should align with what is espoused. For example, if we advocate honesty and integrity in our organizational values, this would mean that we should be mindful of these in all our decision moments.

Given what we have been exploring about learning, habits and patterns, we can suggest that the combination of a number of choices and decisions made by individuals will eventually add up to 'the way things are done around here'. People in an organization will, because of their fundamental need to belong and be accepted, first be inclined to fit in and conform, to work out what is acceptable behaviour in this place and to mirror it. If these behaviour patterns are effective, they will over time become habitual and more hardwired into the deeper parts of the brain (hippocampus), requiring no conscious thought to enact. This happens the world over, from national psyche at a macro level right down to small groups forming in a school community. As a particular behaviour is reinforced by different people throughout the organization it finds its way into training, induction and communications, until it becomes the norm. Until challenged by sufficient numbers or by someone with sufficient weight of influence, the culture will continue to deepen its roots in the system. Over time, these become very strong and will resist change or interference. For example, in the military, presumably in order for people to bond better as units and teams, there are rights of passage and various initiation processes that have been handed down, which are reinforced by a code of behaviour and language that can be quite alien to someone outside that particular world. Over time, these patterns have been found to engender the camaraderie needed in combat and thus are perpetuated. Equally, if you have ever found yourself in an elite sporting establishment or club, it will be made very clear early on what is acceptable and what is not, even down to the dress code. When a culture is well established, there will be formal and informal rules that regulate it. By and large, these will be helpful and become unquestioned second nature for members of the organization. However, as we will see, herein lies the conundrum for responsible leaders, namely, how to encourage proper thoughtfulness and questioning while seeking to bring a consistency of approach that is efficient. Consistent adherence to a good protocol is desirable, whereas blind obedience to a poor rule is not.

Our foundational hypothesis is that a culture of responsibility is based on shared values and perspectives, which in turn promote considered commitment to a wider purpose for the greater good.

For our purposes in this book, I want to identify two seemingly opposing cultures and explore some of the characteristics inherent in each. This might appear rather black and white, but in doing so I want to paint the ends of the continuum, so that as responsible leaders we can then decide for ourselves the cultural flavour we want.

Responsibility from commitment, not compliance: it starts with our view of the world

Figure 6.1 shows two tracks, one that might lead to a responsible outcome and one that might not. There are no certainties in this debate and yet we can be confident that, once on a particular track, it is harder to move from it as it becomes embedded in behaviours.

Track 1: zero-sum game

Track 1 starts with a view of the world that is based on a concept of a zero-sum game in which there are clear winners and losers. Survival of the strongest. The winner takes it all. The objectives in this game are not to lose or be seen heading in that direction. This leads to an orientation of performance as the goal and it is the focus of conversations, meetings, reports and so on. Language used is all about cost and benefit, return on investment, profitability, performance against targets. There is an inherent belief that size is a measure of success and to be the biggest (or first) is desirable. This can result in growth that is not managed or wise, as we saw in Part 1 with the RBS example. As previously stated, there is nothing wrong with performance and competitiveness as neutral forces. What can become destructive, though, is the route that this can take if not handled responsibly. By way of an extrapolation, albeit somewhat extreme, the following could ensue.

At its best, this kind of perspective can lead to creativity and a highly energetic culture. At its worst, however, it can foster an environment in which fear of failure to perform and comparison with others paralyses creativity. Fear is damaging as a state of mind. Neuroscience informs us that when we are fearful we adopt impulsive behaviours driven by the primitive responses of fight or flight. Our study of organizational principles in the brain has revealed that we tend to be in a constant state of flux between how we can minimize danger to ourselves by moving *away from* (pain, which can be physical, emotional and social) and maximize reward by moving *towards* (emotional and satisfaction). Research has discovered that our amygdala (primitive habitual brain) tends to process threat faster than reward, often instantaneously, and that we tend towards a negativity bias, seeing threats as larger than they are.

FIGURE 6.1 A culture continuum

	Orientation	Possible culture	Evidenced by	Role of regulation	Human reactions	When things go wrong	Possible leadership story
TRACK 1 Mindset of Zero sum game Focused on performance	Winners and losers.	Fear generated through fear of failure and comparison.	Defensive behaviours. Protective behaviours. Unhealthy competition. Greed. Under-performance is punished.	To ensure fairness. To control behaviour. To drive compliance. To reduce scope for thinking.	'I resent this.' 'I want to prove myself better than...' 'I want to beat the system.' 'I will do just enough.' 'Everyone else is doing it.' 'I'm tired.'	Blame and accusation. Head burying.	Posturing. Vested interests. Role and status. Same old ideas recycled. Trophy appointments. Process focus.
Short-term focus	Performance as goal	Lip service to moral values	Taking patterns	'We cannot trust you so...'	'Someone else needs to...'	More regulations?	Self-promotional
TRACK 2 Mindset of mutual growth Centred on responsibility	Interdependence.	Respect – even love – through encouragement and appreciation.	Performance through collaboration. Generous behaviours. Learning and curiosity. Responsibility and accountability. Stewardship. Poor performance is explored.	To simplify complexity. To create the environment for growth. To win commitment. To encourage thinking. 'This is for your/our own good.'	'I care about this and its impact on others and the wider system.' 'I think this through carefully.'	Heart searching. Spirit of enquiry and learning.	Ethical and courageous. Responsible. Outcome focus. Actively seeking new faces and new ideas to challenge norms.
Long-term focus	Performance as consequence	Integrity through moral values at the core	Giving patterns	'We want to enable you to...'	'I take full responsibility for my choices'	Refreshing regulations?	Other/wider oriented

What behaviours might this kind of culture engender? Not all of these will manifest and they will not all be extreme, but we have seen in our work examples of the following:

- **Defensive behaviours**: passive aggressive patterns such as agreeing in a meeting and then doing something completely different or undermining decisions; outright aggression to put down underperformers or competitors; withdrawal of support; over-justification of position by proving through ever-increasing volume of evidence of data; requests for more and more data.

- **Protective behaviours**: similar to above, but also including silo thinking and erecting barriers between functions – physical and structural; holding on to information; holding on to talented team members; creating new structures and positions to protect status; denial of truths; hiding of truths and realities.

- **Unhealthy competition** internally and externally: fighting over resources and agenda time; arguing over who owns which success or revenue stream; bending of the rules.

- **Greed**: striving for ever-bigger rewards and bonuses; loss of perspective; trappings of success.

- **Performance is rewarded and underperformance is punished**: league tables; measurement over short timescales, eg daily reporting and weekly reporting; removal of the bottom 10 per cent or equivalent.

- **Narrowness of view**: short-term horizons; internal focus at the expense of customers or end users; disjointed and silo thinking.

- **Lip service to values**: misalignment; fine words that are not supported by actual behaviours; words that do not mean a lot to most people and are not the foundations of 'how things are done'; trite statements that people have heard before and recognize as shallow.

- **'Taking' patterns**: self-focused; possessive; using people; self-promotional; transactional; utility.

- **Stress-related issues**: exhaustion through overwork; long-hours culture; burnout; illusion of busyness; substance abuse to maintain unnatural energy levels; 'never enough'; personal denial and collective collusion with denial (it is not a real problem).

The role of regulation

Within this mindset, there is a need for rules and regulations to ensure fairness and control behaviours, to drive compliance into and throughout the organization and perhaps the wider industry, for example pharmaceuticals or financial services. Rules and compliance are necessary at a foundational level to mitigate danger and clear risks. Speed-limits work, because they reduce accidents and they become habits that as drivers we tend to have embedded into our unconscious competence. However, there is a need to balance the extent to which rules remove the need for an individual to think for themselves about a particular situation. Over-burdensome regulation speaks of a lack of trust and the message received can be as stark as 'I am not trusted to think for myself and my ability to innovate has been taken away from me'. Over the past ten years we have seen a staggering proliferation of rules and regulations in business, education, health sectors, power generation and supply, to name but a few. The roots of this are complex, but the intention is to force people to play by the rules, quite literally.

This thinking does not consider carefully enough the human reactions based on fundamental human needs for fulfilment. Psychologists accept that, as humans, we are intrinsically creative and imaginative. We grow through learning – thinking, feeling, reasoning and evaluating. We are emotional creatures who need to belong *and* who need autonomy to originate for ourselves. We also like to work in like-minded groups. Given this, when presented with what we might judge as excessive regulation or ill-judged controls, it is not surprising that some people will respond resentfully. Other reactions could include:

'I resent this, I'm not trusted any more.'

'This is taking the relationships out of my work – I'm out of here.'

'I want to prove myself better than the system.'

'I want to beat the system.'

'I will do just enough and no more.'

'I'm tired and bored and do not care for the details.'

'Everyone else is doing this and getting away with it, so I might as well too.'

I appreciate that these are extreme statements, but contained in them, if we are honest with ourselves, is the essence of the challenge we set ourselves when we embark on a track like this, focused on performance as the ultimate goal. With a culture in which people pay lip service to values and moral codes (this was present in every financial services business at the time of the crash and existed in BP at the time of the Deep Water Horizon disaster), it is no surprise that our need to fulfil innate ingenuity is fulfilled in self-focused ways. Paying a bribe to secure a contract on favourable terms can be very exhilarating, or fixing an exchange rate to favour a particular trading position causes an adrenaline rush that is highly addictive – and more so if we can get away with it.

And when things go wrong in an organization or an industry like this, the reactions are equally immature. To begin with, blame and accusation. People bury their heads and hide. Regulators impose more rules to counteract what they perceive to be loop holes because things are possibly out of control. And so the cycle goes on.

Leadership in a compliance culture

Leadership in such a culture is about role and status – vested interest. Typically it is about posturing and is territorial, hierarchical and focused in a few individuals. Organizations in the grip of this mindset tend to appoint what might appear to outsiders as trophy appointments into senior executive positions or as board members who will not rock the boat. They recycle old patterns and rely on the past for their credibility. New ideas among leaders are not regarded as important unless the organization has reached a crisis point of poor performance. If this occurs, sadly at the extreme of the continuum with performance as the goal, when new ideas are sought these can be knee jerk and unimaginative, for example slashing a cost base or removing specific functions (outsourcing), or selling off parts of the business. Necessary as these might be, as we will explore later, they tend not to foster a culture of responsibility, instead reinforcing fear and mistrust.

Track 2: mutual growth

Track 2 has a worldview based on a concept that it is possible to enlarge the cake for the mutual benefit of all stakeholders and that both individual and corporate growth is possible, albeit in ways that are more imaginative. A worldview like this is oriented towards interdependence rather than survival of the fittest, as it recognizes that success visits different players in different ways and at different times. Critically, performance is a welcomed consequence of behaviours in this kind of culture, rather than the ultimate and all-consuming goal. Language used is as much long term as it is short term, and will be typified by brand promises, customer loyalty, customer satisfaction, people engagement, product integrity *and* how results are looking. There is a belief in this kind of culture that when the important things are attended to, performance will follow. Furthermore, **this culture looks for ways of measuring success that are more creative than simply financial.** We have seen examples of this already in our journey.

There are potential pitfalls with this kind of culture in that it can become, if poorly led, a place of introspection and even unreality. At worst, such places become so 'cosy' that they can turn into institutions that are passed by. Some colleges and further education establishments have fallen into this trap over the past 20 years or so, being reluctant to evolve with the demands of industries and an expectant public.

However, when well led, a culture on this track is built upon respect, encouragement, learning, value, perhaps even love and genuine affection. This is about a depth of connection to values and a collective story that provides the basis for meaning and purpose. In my work I have come across organizations that have lost their way and, in order to find it again, have been encouraged to return to their roots and heritage to remind themselves of their legacy and draw inspiration from the longer-term narrative. Already we have seen how some banks have had to reconnect with their purpose, having felt that they had lost it in the quest for profit and growth. In the world of motor vehicle manufacturers, Toyota was for many years regarded as the maker of the most reliable cars around. They were not always the most stylish but they never let the driver down. Then things changed. Toyotas began to be recalled in the 2000s and the world wondered why. Incidents of parts failures causing accidents hit the press. This shift coincided with the company's expressed goal to become the world's biggest car manufacturer – to make and sell more cars than anyone else. In so doing, it appeared to many that Toyota took its eye off the ball. Subsequently it has been forced by the power of public opinion to return to its roots of quality and reliability, while also being one of the first manufacturers to develop effective hybrid technology, which incidentally has resulted in the Toyota Prius being one of the most popular hybrid vehicles and one that has set the bar for the future.

On this track, values are not meaningless or trite words. They are fundamental beliefs and are based on a code of moral fibre that includes trust, respect, love, hope and meaning. In his book *Ethicability* (Steare, 2009), Professor Roger Steare presents a clear vision and practical steps for how as individuals and businesses we can be more courageous in stepping away from the crowd and making decisions based on ethical principles, however unpopular they may seem initially. His call for a rediscovery of moral virtues is entirely congruent with our journey towards a responsible culture and is beginning to gain traction in the corporate and political space, albeit not without the expected push-back from those well established on track 1.

What behaviours might this kind of culture engender? As previously with track 1, not all of these will be evident all the time and yet we can identify them from our experience and also the examples (some we have mentioned already) that are becoming increasingly common:

- **Collaborative behaviours**: constructive dialogue and cross-silo thinking and working; genuine desire to break down narrow-minded protectionist barriers; seeking out and welcoming challenge from other sources and departments; discussion with all stakeholders both internal and external.

- **Generous behaviours**: taking the enterprise-wide perspective; sharing knowledge and insights for the wider gain; looking at talent as a resource for the wider organization; being prepared to take a back seat if necessary.

- **Accountability**: positively and proactively supporting corporate decisions that have been reached through proper healthy discussion; taking personal responsibility for actions and choices; raising challenges thoughtfully; holding each other to account for actions and choices upon a foundation of trust and good intention.

- **Creativity and curiosity**: an openness to find new ways of thinking and doing; looking for ideas from imaginative sources; appointments that bring edge and insight.

- **Inclusivity and flexibility**: welcoming diversity of perspective and ideas; adapting structures through a focus on behaviour and mindset rather than changing them constantly.

- **Performance is rewarded, poor performance is explored**: balanced reward for good performance both individually and shared collectively; measurement is over timescales that people can control and fosters longer-term thinking and planning; poor performers are coached where appropriate or redeployed with care; leaders accept responsibility for their part in poor performance.

- **Breadth of view**: long-term horizons; systemic and integrated view across stakeholders.

- **Genuine belief**: alignment behind real values that mean something to all members of the organization; focus on the heritage and story underpinning the organization that provides meaning for people.

- **Giving patterns**: 'otherish' in perspective; stewarding resources wisely; enabling people; relational.

- **Pressure issues**: people working well and willingly under appropriate pressure that is managed; restorative practices in place.

Regulation in this culture

Rules are intended to win commitment rather than enforce compliance. Therefore there is a need to communicate the rationale and secure genuine buy-in to them so that players are clear about why and it makes sense to them. Better still, regulation in this culture helps simplify complexity by cutting through red tape to get to the roots of the issues. Perhaps idealistically, regulations here would be based on ethical and responsible principles such as those introduced by Professor Roger Steare in *Ethicability* (2009) as the **RIGHT** decision-making formula:

- What are the Rules?
- Are we acting with Integrity?
- Who is this Good for?
- Who could we Harm?
- What's the Truth?

As these rules and regulations are based on implicit trust and respect, the response to them is neurologically a 'moving towards' rather than a defensive one. Strange, I know, to be moving towards regulation, but when we know that it is for our (and others') good, it ceases to be a threat or something to defeat. Rules and regulations form the solid foundation upon which we can be more imaginative. One might hear phrases like:

'I care about this and the impact on others and the wider system.'

'I need to think this through carefully.'

'I take full responsibility for my actions and choices.'

'I can hold my head up high on this one.'

'I want to include others in my decision-making processes.'

'Because we know what the right thing to do is, we can focus on developing relationships and moving forward with our clients.'

'Being transparent means we don't waste time and energy justifying everything.'

So, returning to the simple example of being offered a bribe or incentive:

Because I care about the brand reputation of my organization and I can see the negative press coverage ahead, which would require lots of time and effort to justify or refute, I am immediately wary of the offer. I know that there is now an Anti Bribery Act that is targeting this kind of activity. This smells of something that will be contrary to that Act. Then I reflect on the unjust basis that this suggests awarding the business and the impact that this would have on other players in the system who have not taken this route. They would potentially be forced either to adopt these practices, which would itself compound the problem over the long term, or they could be forced out of business. Finally, I might notice that I am reacting emotionally to a bully or a manipulative individual and this reaction is not wholesome for me. Because, as a responsible leader, I work through this thought process, I can come up with the right response and I have not needed reams of regulations.

And when things go wrong in this culture, there is real heart searching, not blame. People feel hurt or disappointed and come together with a spirit of enquiry to learn and explore what behaviours and circumstances led up to the error. They do not default to making more rules; rather, they ask how more responsibility can be taken by more people. It balances a calling forth of something more profound alongside appropriate reprimand.

Leadership in a commitment culture

It follows that leadership in this kind of culture represents all of what we have been exploring so far in the book. Leaders will model responsibility and not be fearful of stepping forward to take courageous decisions. As Margaret Cole from PwC observed, such decisions can sometimes be counter-cultural and appear to be going against the flow, perhaps ethically challenging. Yet responsible leadership is not always about courting controversy or speaking out. Courage could be simply investing in recruiting more graduates when everyone else is cutting back, because it is a long-term view. It can be holding on to people when everyone else is making people redundant. During the recent economic downturn, many large and small businesses have negotiated with their workforce to take pay cuts or extended leave without pay in order to reduce costs while maintaining staffing levels. By doing so, businesses add to their employer brand reputation, which in turn attracts better talent that contributes to performance over the long term. Moreover, they build trust with their people, which reinforces a commitment and responsible culture.

At this point, having described a continuum by looking at both ends, spend a few moments to reflect on the culture that is present in your organization.

Reflections

- What from our descriptions has provoked a reaction for you, both negative and positive? Why?

- How would you describe the culture in your organization as it is now?

- What aspects are both strong and desirable in your view?

- How do these reflect the authentic narrative of the organization?

- How might you want to evolve the culture to make it more commitment based and responsible?

- If you had no restrictions on your actions or choices, what would you do or make happen?

Impacting culture intentionally

Returning to the theme of cultural evolution, we need to be clear how a culture of responsibility will develop and identify the role that we can play intentionally as responsible leaders in facilitating this process. The following are important considerations:

- Cultures evolve one decision and one conversation at a time, over time.
- Distributed leadership is the key to promulgating the story.
- We can identify the 'cool kids' and 'mavericks' to enlist their support.
- The narrative is all-important.

One decision and conversation at a time

When we work with senior leaders we often invite them to define the kind of culture that they want to see in their organization. Almost without exception, this will include the phrase 'a high-performance culture'. As we have discussed, performance as *the* goal is fraught with danger. Performance as a pleasant outcome from attending to other things is certainly worth aspiring for. So we encourage these groups to push deeper and to explore how the culture will be demonstrated. To begin with, we hear phrases like 'people working hard and going the extra mile', 'raising the bar'. Later we hear phrases like 'people doing the right thing' (here it is again...), 'people taking more responsibility for their decisions and actions', 'rewarding for people to work here', 'brave, courageous, confident...'. The list goes on. These are worthy ideals. When we explore how such a culture is developed, sadly there is a paucity of thinking, as leaders believe that, by drafting the statements and cascading a slide deck through presentations and road shows, they will create enough momentum to change the culture. This is only one ingredient.

Culture evolves as a result of individual emotional connections to something deeper, bigger perhaps. As an employee or member of the community, if I choose how I respond in each scenario I encounter, and if I feel at ease or positively stretched (not threatened), inspired or enlarged, I am more likely to respond favourably. As already mentioned, if values and norms in the community align with my personal paradigms, the connections are cemented more permanently. For example, if my boss encourages me and supports me to present the findings of my research to a senior executive team because it is my work and she believes in it (and me), then, although it might be a daunting prospect at first, I feel great when it goes well and I form a hypothesis that the culture in her team is one of stretch and support. It is also clear that she is fostering responsibility on my part.

When we work with teams that want to create a high-performance culture, one area of focus is the nature of the conversations that take place at important moments and around significant processes in the wider system we introduced in Part 1. To create a responsible culture, these conversations are meaningful and intentional. This means that people plan well for them and, where necessary, rehearse them ahead of time. Where there is limited time for preparation, parties in the conversation use skilled noticing and listening in the moment to remain intentional throughout. Here are some important moments that have a significant impact on culture:

- recruitment and induction of new team members;
- performance management discussions;
- promotion interviews and talent management discussions;
- coaching discussions;
- customer sales presentations;
- handling customer complaints and problems;
- briefings to the press, analysts and wider market;
- senior leaders' contact with, and briefings to, teams across the organization;

- internal presentations with executive committees;
- team meetings and management meetings.

To improve the quality of these conversations, consider:

- How clear is the principal message for the conversation? (It is best to avoid lengthy meetings with too many points of discussion, as this dilutes impact and increases the potential for confusion based on tiredness. All-day meetings are common in business and not very effective.)
- How can you ensure that the content of the discussion is focused on the key message(s)?
- How can you ensure the quality of the listening by all parties?
- How can you set a pace that is both focused and allows for real thinking?
- What can you do to make the conversation a generative one that moves things forward?
- How can you be responsible for holding parties accountable for responses and actions?
- How will you ensure that decisions taken are mindful of the wider system and longer term as well as short term?
- How will the organization's values be demonstrated openly and authentically in the conversation?

By way of example, I have heard of many occasions, and been part of them myself, when senior leaders have prepared for an important client meeting at the last minute, in the taxi on the way to the session. This may seem like good use of time, but when there is a more junior member of the team present in the taxi who might be feeling anxious about saying the right things at the right time, this behaviour sets an irresponsible tone. It demonstrates an arrogance of approach ('I can wing this if I need to') and is disrespectful to clients (what would they say if they knew how preparation was done?) and it models behaviours that are unprofessional. It would be unthinkable for a surgeon not to look at X-rays and case notes, and then fail to meet a patient before an operation. And yet, in some business circles, arrogance still prevails.

Another trend of our modern revolution is the proliferation of information and data, which in turn exerts a force on leaders that says to them that they have to be in touch and accessible all the time. A positive role model I encountered was a regional operational director in Canada for a global business, who stipulated that no e-mails should be sent between 2.00 pm on a Friday and 9.00 am on a Monday by people in her function. Initially this was received with great scepticism, but over time people welcomed the pause and were able to have meaningful and creative conversations on Fridays as well as giving quality attention to their families and friends.

Leaders can set the tone for great conversations and in so doing empower people in their teams to do likewise. They do not have to evolve the culture single-handedly, merely to recognize that their behaviour is watched and copied throughout.

Distributed leadership

It follows, therefore, that to develop a responsible culture, senior leaders acknowledge that they have a profoundly important role in setting tone and modelling behaviour, and then they call up leadership from all levels in the organization to be accountable.

When there is little fear present in an organization, people feel freer to take up responsibility and personal accountability. Moreover, this is not just in the role of team managers or leaders; each person is responsible for his or her choices and is therefore a responsible leader *for* the organization.

This is not to do away with management. Managers will always be necessary throughout a system to monitor and keep things on track day to day. No, what we are talking about here is how the culture facilitates each and every person to feel that he or she can and should influence the impact that the organization has through his or her personal leadership in the moment. One description that might apply is that of ambassadors for the organization. So rather than working *in* the organization or indeed working *for* someone, employees are encouraged to view themselves as custodians of the brand and the culture. In Part 1 we encountered Marriott Hotels and The John Lewis Partnership, businesses that have distributed leadership responsibility to the point of contact with the customer. Where people feel genuine connection to the values and narrative, individually, leadership can happen anywhere. When companies are looking for engagement, this is what they prize highly – a kind of affection for the company and what it stands for and a willingness to lead where you are.

When looking to build such a culture, the temptation is to start with the top, as we have seen, and to dictate what the new or changed culture is going to be. While setting the tone at the top is vital, the real evolution happens at all the levels in the business. A top-down cascade process reinforces the old thinking and hierarchy. It assumes that senior leaders know the answers and that they can give permission for people further down the organization to adopt newly agreed ways of working. Given what we have been discussing about leading in the new world, the need to challenge assumptions and paradigms, forward-thinking organizations challenge this, carefully. They look to start culture evolution journeys throughout the organization, often simultaneously. Working with the 'middles' and 'emerging leader population' will create healthy, if challenging, pressure for changes upwards and downwards. More importantly, it sends messages of openness to ideas, inclusion and valuing contribution. It flies in the face of the cynics who would dismiss talk of different ways of working as 'not invented here' or 'simply mandated upon us without being consulted'. Remember, as human beings we are resourceful. We relish the opportunity to be creative and to innovate. And we prefer a degree of autonomy within something to which we can say we belong. A wise responsible leader will recognize these factors and work with them, not against them.

Some years ago, I was working with a medium-sized charity that was going through a significant upheaval and repositioning of its brand. This charity had been around for over 150 years and had a simple mission over that time. However, the world was changing and the organization needed to adapt its offering, think about how it connected with its donors, and tell its story in a more relevant way. The CEO realized, with his senior team, that this would involve significant changes both structurally and behaviourally. He wanted people to feel part of the new shape of the charity and so began a series of whole-system workshops in which members of the executive team were joined by people from all levels in the business to explore the future together. Each workshop had between 20 and 30 participants and time was spent in small groups, pairs and as a whole, discussing, experiencing and playing. Stories of the past, what had been achieved and why people felt attached to the past were shared openly, as were ideas for how the charity could move forward. I recall the moment when the CEO sat in the same discussion group as the lady who ran the post room, and they argued quite forthrightly about a new structure. Then they hugged each other as they found a form of agreement, built on their belief in the charity and what its larger purpose was. The whole process was about people individually feeling part of, and accountable for (responsible), the long-term survival and success of the charity. The CEO did effect the changes in the culture over a two-year period with the help of the whole business before he moved on, having done his work. The charity is still going strong and fulfilling its mission, having gained a reputation for being more forward thinking than many in the sector imagined.

Working with the 'cool kids'

I was asked by a senior executive, of a global financial services business that was in difficulty, how they could change the culture in the business. The markets were pressurizing them to demonstrate that they were taking seriously the messages they had been given by the press, the public and the regulator. We agreed that culture was about behaviours and that the business had got used to some bad ones that had gone unchecked for many years. Different parts of the business had completely different cultures and viewed each other with huge suspicion and derision. The 'they' had become pervasive, as few people were taking responsibility for their individual actions or decisions. Someone else should shoulder the responsibility and blame. I suggested that the evolution would take time and that it could not be achieved with just a simple 'sheep dip' (where all employees are mandated to attend the same programme over a short period) of all staff (over 100,000 globally). That might be necessary to kick things off, but what would be needed would be as much viral as it would be structured. It would require working with and through the 'cool kids' in the organization.

To define 'cool kids', it is helpful to use a simple framework (see Figure 6.2). This is a commonly used framework for defining some types of people in an organization. It is crude, yet can be very valuable. By asking to what extent

FIGURE 6.2 Identifying the 'cool kids'

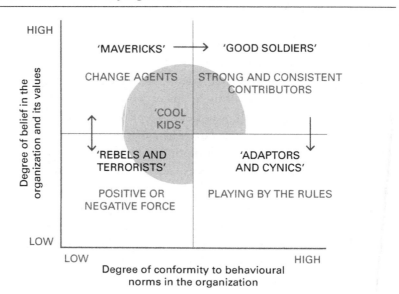

people believe in the organization and what it stands for, and then asking them to what extent they feel that they can and do conform to the behavioural norms, some generic groupings are formed.

There are those who toe the line and play by the rules without really buying into the values of the organization. We call these 'adaptors' at best or, at worst, they can be 'cynics' who will merely bide their time. All organizations have some of these people. They can be harmless if they are not vocal and lie low for many years. But equally they can be dangerous if they become generators of negative energy as cynics.

There are those who are strong and consistent contributors who both believe in the business and conform to behavioural norms. We call these 'good soldiers', which is a somewhat pejorative term to label what one would hope would be the bulk of the workforce.

The two remaining groups are in many ways the most interesting when thinking about culture evolution and change. The group that includes people who believe in what the organization stands for but do not conform to norms of behaviour are likely to comprise many of the people who want to change things and look for new ways of working. They are unorthodox change agents, although the term used is 'maverick'. We all know these people. They try new ways of doing things and want to impact the business – positively – because they believe in it. They are difficult to lead or manage because they challenge assumptions or traditions. They can be described as 'edgy'. What is important to notice, though, is that all organizations need these people from time to time, as they provide the catalyst energy for change and evolution. They will prevent institutionalization.

Finally, there are those who no longer believe in the values or conform to behaviours. These have become rebels or terrorists. Again, most organizations will have some of these. They may have outlasted their time with the company and be ready to move on, through disillusionment or boredom perhaps. For whatever reason, though, it is important for leaders to be mindful of this group and its potential for both good and harm. If cynics become embittered, they can slip into the role of terrorist – someone who will actively work against the system to thwart it. This is harmful and undermines the culture. On the other hand, if mavericks become frustrated, say by the pace of change, they may become a rebel and begin to lose their positive energy. These people need careful and quick handling by leadership to restore them to a more positive position.

In an ideal world, mavericks will evolve into good soldiers, perhaps for a long time, but often this is true only for a shorter time, as their fulfilment is typically in the catalyst role. However, retaining mavericks is difficult, as the system will eventually want them to conform or eject them. Leaders who recognize this and manage it wisely are indeed responsible leaders, as they have identified the value of having sufficient mavericks and, if need be, replenishing them, especially in tough or ambiguous times. It is these people who will provoke responses to tough questions.

So what has this to do with 'cool kids'? Classic change theory advises us as leaders to identify change agents and early adopters. This is fine, but limits our thinking. One difficulty is that it can also be seen as the usual approach and is open to abuse. For example, it is not uncommon for an ambitious 'maverick' to continually volunteer to be a change champion in order to garner favour with the leadership and thus lose his or her authenticity, which teams then see through as shallow and the change is not adopted, as they perceive it as something to which they are just paying lip service. No, in the modern world, the 'cool kids' are those individuals who are followed or who can gather a crowd (actual or virtual). 'Cool kids' have views and opinions that are worth listening to and they have the attractive assuredness that we identified in Part 1 to contribute in an understated yet impactful way.

They are likely to be found located somewhere around the maverick, rebel and good soldier region of our diagram. They will not be negative cynics or passive adaptors. Nor will they be totally compliant or hell-bent on subversion. But they will believe in the organization sufficiently strongly to want to improve it and to see it thrive in the modern world. *And* they will be happy to step forward and take responsibility for shifting a small part of it.

'Cool kids' are found at all levels in an organization. How do you identify them? There is no magic formula. In the 21st century we should now be comfortable with the requirement to look beyond our normal paradigms and keep an open mind as to who the agents for change might be. Nonetheless, as we are talking about developing a culture of responsibility, we can be on the lookout for some qualities and behaviours. We identified some of these in Part 1 and, ideally, senior leaders and those charged with developing people and managing the talent agenda in the business should be using these as a backdrop to many conversations.

Here are some other possible patterns to notice about 'cool kids':

- They are often reluctant leaders with a degree of natural humility that attracts people from all different genres.
- They are not superior in their attitude.
- People seem to want to go the extra mile for them without needing to be told or invited.

- They bring people together around a cause or an initiative easily, eg social, volunteering, new ideas.
- They are accountable themselves and those around them find it easy to be accountable as well, for both successes and failures.
- The climate around them is infectious, often fun and energetic, and always positive – 'what we could do', 'imagine if'.
- They offer suggestions and ways through situations.
- Their language is encouraging and talks of belief and affirmation.

Formal and emergent

As we become more comfortable with emerging changes and evolution of the responsible agenda, we can allow both formal change programmes and informal viral progress to coexist and complement each other. So in the example of the financial services business needing to rediscover a responsible agenda, the initial wholesale 'sheep dip' would only gain traction if supported by genuine conversations that are locally relevant rather than a formal dictate about how people should behave. After all, this organization was not brought lower by the majority of the workforce, who are 'good soldiers' and were stunned to discover that one arm of the business was contemptuous of the rest and behaving as uncontrolled rebels and terrorists. To chastise the whole business would risk betraying the goodwill and trust of most of its people. 'Cool kids' are able to help make sense of the current situation and the future direction locally for different teams and groups. Using thinking around the wider system and aligning with the core beliefs of people (and the business), they can encourage people to talk openly about the impact on customers or how to become better at collaborating with other parts of the business or how certain ethical decisions are handled. They naturally see the value in bringing together a cross-section of hierarchy and silos into an open conversation to tackle the tough questions. And the role of leaders is to give them space and to trust that they will light small fires – beacons – around the organization that become visible to others, such that people will start to ask about what is happening in such and such department. Stories of a different approach will begin to be shared virally.

By way of example, allow me to reintroduce you to Richard Oldfield, a senior partner at PwC. Fundamentally a 'maverick' at heart, he became a partner when he was in his very early thirties and had a reputation then as an energetic and enthusiastic guy. I recall him coming to see me and wanting to discuss how he could have impact now as a junior partner.

We discussed his motivation for this and it soon became clear that he wanted to find ways to inspire the generations behind him, whom he regarded as talented and in need of leadership that was able to relate closely to them. He decided that he did not need permission to bring together a group of younger people with potential, so he advised his seniors in the partnership what he was intending to do and why. Soon thereafter he had personally invited a dozen or so emerging talent, most of whom were strong performers and people with ideas to shape the business's future (mavericks and good soldiers), to a lunch and afternoon discussion at a top city hotel. He wanted them to feel special and that their views and contribution were valued. He repeated the gathering on a few more occasions and soon the group was generating ideas for wider consideration in the business. Richard sowed a view of inclusion and openness that began to be modelled by the group themselves. Some of that group attended the Responsible Leadership Programme that we encountered in Chapter 5, and most have gone on to become partners in the organization where they continue to model 'cool kid' behaviours. Richard has himself gone on to become a senior figure in the business and has championed a responsible leadership agenda through his work with clients and emerging leaders in the business. He is also one of a number of leaders and staff at PwC who are actively involved in the local and wider community.

Reflections

- To what extent are people in your organization encouraged to lead where they are at their level, irrespective of status or position?

- If not, what stops you and the organization from allowing people to step forward to lead, however small or large the role?

- How can you identify the 'cool kids', 'mavericks' and helpful 'rebels' in your organization?

- How can you ensure that they are enabled to seize the responsible agenda and begin to light fires locally through role-modelling new ways of working?

- What barriers do you foresee to fostering a culture in which formal change programmes are supported by emergent initiatives?

The narrative is all-important

Weaving all these threads together is a critical act of responsible leadership. If culture is *how things are done around here*, it is vital that the cumulative effect of individual conversations and decisions happens against a backdrop of a coherent and compelling narrative that answers the questions *'Why are we doing this?'* *'What's the joined-up story behind all this?'*

We might wonder why this is important for people, and Figure 6.3 illustrates this simply. This is a model that we use with many of our clients and, without exception, people are quick to relate to it in their situation.

Underpinning this is a key principle that people want to, and need to, connect with an organization or a cause at four levels. Responsible leaders pay attention to each of these separately and consider them as a whole, for it is this that ensures that change is more lasting.

Working from the outer ring inwards, first the connection is at the **body** level and this has to do with how people apply insights in their roles. It is

FIGURE 6.3   Lasting change

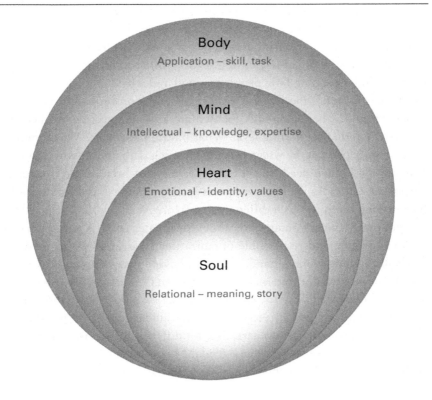

about what they do, what skills they have and how they use them. This level is where capability and competency frameworks can be very helpful, as they set out for people components of their roles and inform training plans. Simply put, this is about *practical outworking*.

The next level inwards is the connection at the **mind** level and this has to do with what people know, *cognitively and intellectually*. Our modern world values knowledge, and many businesses now base their unique differentiation on this. Large premiums can be necessary to attract expertise (and retain it), and this occurs in most sectors now, from the charity and not-for-profits through to retail, finance and professional services.

These two levels are where most organizations have traditionally focused much of their energy and budget over the past 30 years. Competitive advantage has been about attracting the people with the right knowledge and ensuring that they can apply this quickly and effectively. Training programmes have been targeted at developing skills. Assessment centres have been used to determine whether someone is competent across a range of capabilities for the role level they are being asked to perform. These foci are not wrong. But as we are seeing, in the modern VUCA world, they represent only half the picture and it is in the other levels that more lasting connections are made.

At the **heart** level, people are connecting with their values and their identity. This is tapping into the *emotional* aspects of our humanity and we have touched on these a lot during this book. Neuroscience research is now informing so much more of responsible leaders' thinking as they become more fluent in understanding how people respond and why.

At the **soul** level, the focus is *relational* – relationships right across the wider system. To be relationally focused means to connect with others and the system and at a meaning level. What binds us together? What connects us with other parts of the wider system? Meaning is about the 'why' question. It is a basic human need that for decades has not been at the core of the corporate world. As we have seen, this is now changing and astute leaders have woken up to this as a differentiator. Moreover, they have realized that it is not just about advantage, it is about the greater good. A paradigm shift.

A compelling and responsible organizational narrative works across all levels in this simple model and, importantly, references the inner two rings openly for internal and external people. Stephen Denning, in his inspirational work *The Leader's Guide to Storytelling: Mastering the art and discipline of business narrative* (2011), provides helpful guidance on constructing and delivering a range of business narratives for different scenarios. As we explore the need for a more responsible agenda, I want to draw on his work and highlight some likely components of such a narrative:

1 To acknowledge where things are currently at – what is good and what is less so and what each and everyone of us has contributed.

2 To whet people's appetite for what a positive different and evolving future might look like and feel like, using powerful yet realistic language.

3 To place all the participants in the story as active players contributing to this future and to call out from them responsibility and ownership for action.

4 If possible, refer to steps that have actually happened or examples where progress has been made already, so that players are encouraged to believe it possible.

5 Construct individual scenarios of the new world that bring the future to life for stakeholders.

A narrative is more than just a vision statement. It guides and acts as a plumbline for decisions and behaviours, as a thread or series of threads coursing throughout the veins of the business.

Here are two examples drawn from very different organizations. The first is from Unilever, which we have mentioned previously. Its Project Sunlight initiative taps into the heritage of the business – Port Sunlight is the spiritual home of the business where the Lever brothers established the initial production facilities now replicated all over the world. It focuses on how the business can galvanize people the world over behind the narrative of creating a better future for children. The website (often now the main vehicle for delivering stories) contains a myriad of positive stories illustrating how small acts of responsibility (sunlight) combine to make the vision reality via a genuine movement that allows anyone and everyone to participate. As a narrative it commits the organization to live this out in its choices on the ground and the organization ties its products into the narrative.

Unilever: Project Sunlight

We believe there has never been a better time to create a brighter future for our children; a world where everyone has enough food to eat and no child goes to bed hungry.

Where every child reaches their fifth birthday and has the right to a happy childhood.

Where every home has enough water to drink and to wash, cook and clean.

And where everybody can enjoy life today while protecting the planet for future generations.

Project Sunlight is a movement that has already started.

It's made up of a growing community of people who believe it is possible to build a world where everyone lives well and lives sustainably.

Who recognize we can only achieve this if we all work together to do small actions every day that make a real difference.

And who inspire others to join us in making this the way everyone chooses to live.*

The second is from the Eden Project, a truly remarkable project to create the world's largest biospheres within a redundant quarry in Cornwall and to use them to build an educational movement that encourages generations to steward resources carefully. The words below are taken from the Guide given to all visitors to the venue and form the introduction by Sir Tim Smit, the founder of Eden. The booklet is itself the complete narrative, showing as it does in imaginative ways the variety of methods the project is using to inspire generations:

Eden Project

Welcome to Eden.

Eden is about optimism and the possibility of change. It is about the fragility of certainty and the feet of clay we all suffer from, but it is also about attitude. Our attitude is simple and infuses everything we do. Come here to remember our connection to nature and our dependence on it for all we need.

Those Biomes you see, those magnificent plants and the accompanying paraphernalia of art, artefact and artifice are simply there to remind us that when we work with the grain of nature, the miracle of the living systems that provide for us on this beautiful planet of ours is both humbling and inspiring. 'Reasonable men bend themselves to the ways of the world, therefore it stands to reason that only the unreasonable can change it,' said Mark Twain. Eden isn't a bohemian enclave apart from the world; it is populated by realists who dared to be passionately unreasonable. Our work with communities across the country and abroad shows how quickly change can be made to happen when people work together. As we face perhaps some of the most challenging times in our history, I feel we were made for this moment.

In our next phase, we are fizzing with ideas for extending and improving Eden, the visitor attraction. Beyond that, our ambition is to play a major role in effecting social and environmental change locally, nationally and internationally. Unreasonable? I don't think so.

Since it opened in 2001, the Eden Project has welcomed millions of visitors to its inspirational venue. Moreover, it is working throughout the world, educating communities and playing its responsible part in shaping a different future.

* Reproduced with kind permission of Unilever and group companies

These two examples illustrate the value of crafting language to reflect the organizational values and the bigger story while inviting stakeholders to play their part and take responsibility.

Reflections

- Thinking about your own organization, how clear and inspirational is the current narrative?

- To what extent does it call people towards a positive future?

- How can you include different stakeholders in the narrative and speak to responsibility on their part?

- How can your narrative connect across body, mind, heart and soul?

- Where can you look for inspiration from other sources?

Summary

During this chapter we have explored how to evolve a culture of responsibility, first by noticing the difference between two examples of a culture, one built on a mindset of a zero-sum game and one built on a mindset of mutual growth. In each of these we identified typical behaviours, the role of regulation and the nature of leadership. Secondly, we highlighted ways in which a responsible culture can be intentionally shaped:

- by focusing on how significant conversations throughout the organization can be more meaningful and foster accountability;

- by recognizing and promoting leadership throughout all levels of the organization and beginning to impact culture by bringing together groups from across the system;

- by encouraging the tone from the top of the organization to enable and release leaders;

- by identifying who the change agents are in the system and specifically who the 'cool kids' are, and then intentionally enlisting their energy and support (formally and informally) to bring about the evolution;

- by focusing on building a compelling, inspiring and inclusive narrative that connects across body, mind, heart and soul for people.

These insights are not the only ways to change or evolve a culture. They represent a little of what I and others are beginning to discover about how organizations and leaders behave in the modern world. If we are to respond to the revolution and the cry for responsibility, we will need to pay attention to the details and to ask the tough questions of ourselves and our colleagues. As Einstein so profoundly observed, to challenge our thinking also and what that might mean for our behaviours.

In the next chapter, we will identify some pitfalls that might await us and some myths that we need to slay to embed the changes we aspire to see.

Potential pitfalls and myths

07

> *Leadership is a potent combination of strategy and character. But if you must be without one, be without the strategy.* **(GENERAL NORMAN SCHWARZKOPF)**

In the previous chapter we examined some ways in which we can evolve a more responsible culture and the reader might be forgiven for thinking it was as straightforward as that. Unfortunately it is not so. What we do know is that many organizations, large and small, are trying to move along this continuum, with mixed success. Those that are committed to it are learning as organizations and are beginning to notice that some of the traditional levers that they choose to use to enable the transition are less effective nowadays.

This chapter will highlight four assumptions (perhaps myths) that I believe need careful attention if we are to be successful on this, bringing about lasting change. This is not an exhaustive list, and for your own organization they may or may not apply. However, in the spirit of openness and curiosity, let us consider how:

- we can go beyond just saying the words;
- we can see further than simply a restructuring;
- we can avoid always promoting the usual suspects;
- we can resist the temptation to measure people into submission.

Just saying the words does not equal progress or change

At the end of the last chapter we encountered two examples of a narrative that seemed to capture the essence of a responsible mindset and inspire stakeholders towards a different future. And these are fine words, inspirational to many. However, they are just words. They will tap into a deeper level of emotional meaning for people, but this will only become impactful if they are supported by aligned activity.

Over many years, business schools and writers have urged leaders to generate vision statements, mission statements and values statements that appear in annual reports, on websites, on posters around offices, on mouse mats at desks and on apps on tablets. Not surprisingly, many of these contain words and phrases that we have mentioned already, such as:

- integrity, honesty, trust, excellence, teamwork, customer-focused, innovation, creativity, doing the right thing, courageous and so on;
- to be the best in... to be number one in... to be the most highly respected...

Sadly, many of us who are employees, customers or observers have developed a kind of healthy (perhaps unhealthy in some cases) indifference to these, which if reinforced might also slip into cynicism. We have grown tired of these words as they have been proven to be empty, as businesses, politicians, public figures and leaders have fallen short of them.

Getting beneath the surface

What is required is for organizations to spend some time and energy going beneath the surface to discover what such statements will and do (these are *very* different verbs) mean in practice. And a myth that is worth highlighting here is that **even though words can be aspirational and desirable, it does not automatically mean that they are being modelled.**

For example, I was working with a group of emerging leaders in Germany and the topic of honesty came up as a core value and distinctive for them as a business. I reminded them that to be dishonest would never appear on any company's list of values and so it was hardly a differentiating factor. We then explored what it meant in practice, with some alarming results. The group was posed a challenge:

> You have been asked to tender for a large piece of work with a client, which you are keen to win. You know you do not have the expertise in house at the moment to do this work and that were you to win it, you would not have the capacity in the existing team to deliver it on time and to a high quality. Moreover, to pitch for the work will require a lot of effort and could impact delivery of work on existing projects. What do you do?

Without exception, the group said they would continue to pitch for the work. They would find a way of delivering it if they won. The group was challenged about how honest this was being to the existing clients whose projects might suffer, and how honest they were being with the potential client about their levels of expertise or capacity. The response was that they would not need to bring this to their attention for fear of sowing doubt. Then there was the question about how honest they were being with the existing team members, who would be required to work longer and harder to deliver the pitch and, if they won the work, to accommodate it within their work levels. This dilemma proved a tough one, as the group split between those who would involve team members in the decision whether to proceed or not, and those who would go ahead and simply allocate new tasks to people. What was clear was that it was easy to say the word 'honesty' and have it as a value, but that it required deeper thought and could mean tough choices in practice. And yet honesty is only a value when it does impact decisions and actions.

Where leaders have engaged with stakeholders, and especially team members, to explore what values will require people to do *and* not do on the ground, there is always a shift in ownership and responsibility. Courageous leaders are open to finding ways through tough dilemmas *with* their people. Mindful of the neuroscience insights we have mentioned already, they ask people for real scenarios that have been encountered and then they take the time to unpick them, aware that it is the emotional connections alongside the analytical ones that shape real behaviour change, not just the cognitive. Furthermore, where there is no obvious or right answer, they make it possible for their people to operate within the ambiguity without fear of punishment.

Avoiding over-communication

Consistently, I find that the word 'communication' is an answer to the question 'what do we need to do more of or get better at?' And yet when we enquire of clients what it is that gets in the way of their ability to execute plans and do the work, often the response is 'too many e-mails or requests for information'. We will deal with the latter point later in this chapter, but the former is illustrative of another myth of leadership and culture, namely that the more leaders communicate, the more people will take on board the messages and change behaviours.

In a world of information overload, we have already highlighted that hearing through the noise is a mark of responsible leadership and it follows that we should not therefore contribute intentionally to adding to the volume of noise, thereby making it harder for our people to hear what is really important. Regrettably, the opposite is often the case. Because leaders feel that their message has not been taken on board they revert to saying it more or, metaphorically, louder. They send out more cascades to teams, more slide decks, more reminders. They appoint more local champions to talk through the communication packs. I have encountered leaders who felt obligated to tweet daily to their teams because this was clearly the thing to be seen to be doing. Psychologically, this has the effect of numbing recipients to what could be important, as they are inclined to ignore frequent and superficial messages. Worse still, it can feel like a Big Brother presence. Oddly, a boss passing a desk and asking spontaneously how things are going is something we are more likely to welcome.

This phenomenon is especially true now in the world of geographically dispersed teams, or teams in which many people work from home. Leaders have encountered the challenge of how to make communication work over distances or where they do not actually meet people face to face. There is no easy answer to this. As a generation we are collectively exploring this dilemma and we need to remain open to careful thought around the issues. Here we can employ some of the learning from earlier chapters, particularly around the nature of listening and effective dialogue.

One of my coaching clients had a team that was located in different countries and time zones. He held regular monthly calls with the team, but was frustrated by the lack of participation and the quality of the conversations. Too often he found himself doing most of the talking, and he found it hard to bring certain individuals into the discussion. When we explored the nature of the monthly calls – what they were trying to achieve and what the subject matter was – it became clear that they were trying to do everything in one session, including catch-up, information giving, performance updates and decisions about rollout of new initiatives. It was no wonder that these lengthy calls bored people and as only one sense was being used – audio – it was difficult for people to read what was going on (not to mention the occasional language misunderstanding). But my client was clear that he did not want to hold even more calls with the whole team, and he was correct in that. It would merely add to the volume.

What he was struggling with was the need to find the right blend of frequency, content and quality of communication. He was mixing surface-level communication with deeper and important messages. His team was confused about how to respond to information dumps or messages about culture change, all in the same discussion. If we adopt the principles discussed earlier, my client needed to reach out to individuals one to one first, so that he and they could cultivate a deeper understanding of each other at the core level and build mutual trust. Once trust is built, it becomes easier to have less frequent but more meaningful interactions more quickly. Doing this for each member of his team, either through one-to-one video calls or ideally at face-to-face encounters, meant that when they came together the ground work had been done with him and he would be able to encourage them individually and collectively to take more ownership. Also, during the monthly calls he began to strip away the superficial items or the informational updates, freeing up time to get to important and deeper matters earlier. This required people to be responsible themselves for seeking out beforehand what information they felt they needed, rather than for him to feel he had to control the information they got. My client realized that **change comes through the quality of the discussion and how it focuses on important priorities or challenging thinking, for example, rather than through frequency of contact and control of information.** If he was seeking to encourage more local accountability and responsibility, he needed to give away some of his control and have less frequent but more impactful conversations. He was pleased to report that the quality of the calls changed, and that when he visited the regions the nature of the one-to-one discussions became very fruitful and mutually beneficial.

Properly aligning reward, recognition and performance management to responsibility

I want to make a key observation concerning one important lever to embed cultural change, namely the role of performance management. **It is important to think beneath the obvious apparent benefits of linking reward overtly to performance if you are looking to foster responsibility.** We have seen already that an over-focus on performance can create a fear of failure or an overly competitive culture. And yet businesses remain wedded to performance-related pay and forced distribution curves (where a fixed percentage of people are required to be rated at the top, a fixed percentage in the middle, and a fixed percentage – usually 10 per cent – rated poor performers), seemingly ignorant of the divisive impact this has on the culture and, ironically, performance.

The argument goes something like this:

If we incentivize people with sufficient reward we will motivate them to work harder and perform better. The best will rise to the top and the poorest performers will be identified and we can remove them. We will reward the top performers financially with a bonus. The middle rump of our business will continue to operate as before and be inspired to aspire for the bigger bonus, but be wary of falling into the bottom 10 per cent for fear of being exited. Therefore they will work harder and in so doing the overall performance of the organization will improve. (Jack Welch famously espoused this approach at GE and it has been adopted by many ambitious companies and leaders since.)

This is old thinking and will not help us thrive in the new world. In *Drive* (2009), Daniel Pink confronts this thinking by showing that as humans we are motivated by autonomy, mastery and purpose – words that we have ourselves touched upon during this book. Pink identifies our fixation on external motivators such as control and reward. This concept is flawed, as it implies that *I* as a leader can motivate *you*, my team member, to do something or be better through an external factor that *I* control. This creates dependency, not responsibility. Neuroscience teaches us now that we motivate ourselves through our choices based on the outcome we seek. So if we want to move away from pain (perhaps being shouted at in a meeting or victimized as being underperforming), we either withdraw or fight back through defensive behaviours (blame, for example) or extra effort, or at worst, bending the rules to achieve a target. Alternatively, we might want to move towards the feeling of being top of the class. This may indeed work in the short term, but it is not creating positive connections in our brains based on a wider perspective of the system. It serves to narrow the focus on 'me'. Pink's study also found that financial reward was very unlikely to motivate people to perform better.

He shows us that as humans we seek autonomy – to be in control of our own environment, and when given sufficient empowerment (through space to operate, time to do it, freedom to choose the way we do it and autonomy over our team), we are motivated *and* typically outperform those for whom the opposite conditions apply. He identifies that what drives us is our desire to learn and to master ourselves and our innate talents so that we can be in the flow (in 'our element' – see Part 1). This taps into creativity and innovation, and our willingness to invest effort. Furthermore, according to Pink, it is a sense of purpose (perhaps bigger purpose) – the reason why we are doing something – that can be a game changer:

> Autonomous people working toward mastery perform at very high levels. But those who do so in service of some greater objectives can achieve even more. The most deeply motivated people – not to mention those who are most productive and satisfied – hitch their desires to a cause larger than themselves.

This suggests that as leaders we need to be more creative about performance management and reward in particular. If we are espousing a responsible culture that strives to do the right thing for our various worlds, it cannot be true that this always equals rewarding only the highest scorers or removing the weakest links based on a league table of points. Furthermore, in times when bonuses cannot be paid because, say, market conditions have contrived against a business or sector, if we have focused on this as the only performance lever to date, we as leaders will be found wanting and bereft of ideas. In such conditions, a forced distribution curve will appear empty and simply be a consumer of time and effort. I have met many leaders in organizations who complain to me, as an external consultant, that they spend weeks of their time each year trying to evaluate performance, fit it into an expected model and then placate all the people whom it fails to satisfy. They find it unfulfilling, stressful, demotivating and ultimately a distraction from the real purpose they signed up for.

We need to be innovative, focus more on recognition and think courageously about resisting the pressure to link reward to performance tables. When we focus on recognition, we open up a new domain of leadership that is more spontaneous, authentic, inspiring and far less time consuming.

Recognition is behavioural, not a process. When we notice effort, a willingness to learn, a desire to go the extra mile, brilliant customer handling, time spent to coach a colleague, an unconditional offer of a creative new idea to solve a problem or a gentle encouragement, we are faced with a leadership moment. We can store it up for an end-of-period review or we can acknowledge the behaviour there and then, stressing the importance of contributing to the longer-term sustainability of the team or organization. When we do this as leaders, the behaviour is noticed by our people and begins to evolve the culture towards responsibility rather than dependence.

Other ways to recognize contribution can include:

- writing thought leadership pieces;
- press coverage of achievements;
- opportunities to share and speak at conferences;
- personal development via a full range of learning opportunities;
- arranging secondments to clients or different sectors;
- responsible leadership secondments to the third sector;
- involvement in exciting and stretching new projects.

Certainly recognition *can* involve awards. I recently attended one such awards ceremony recognizing excellence in leadership in the health sector. Some critics suggested that the money and time spent on this gathering could have been better spent. I disagree; it could have been spent differently, of course, but in a sector that is consistently being challenged to deliver more for less and where leadership is under huge scrutiny in the public gaze, it was surely worthwhile to bring people together to share ideas and learning, while recognizing individuals who have inspired others locally through responsible leadership in action.

Consider for a moment the not-for-profit and social enterprise sector. Here we find motivated individuals often working long hours and introducing creative ideas that have lasting impact on communities the world over. It would be tough to find someone in this sector going the extra mile for the promise of a financial or performance bonus. For them, purpose is all-important. These organizations have no choice other than to look to recognition. For them also, simple words on paper do not count for much. It is collective action that defines them and leadership that enables this to happen.

As we conclude this short section, here are some further reflections:

Reflections

- How can you and your organization ensure that you make it possible for your people to make sense of values and vision words for themselves, and give them the time and space to do this?

- What traps do you or might you fall into around communication in your team or organization?

- How can you be more imaginative about aligning performance management more closely with the dimensions of a responsible culture?

Restructuring alone will not yield results

Now that we are more aware of the emotional impact that our leadership decisions might have on our people, and the part that this plays in motivation to perform, it is still surprising how often leaders omit to consider this when embarking on a restructuring exercise to bring about changes, efficiencies or improvements. I have encountered leaders who are frustrated that despite introducing new roles or streamlining the structure, 'they are still not getting it and are not doing what I want them to be doing. They don't seem to want to take responsibility.' This reveals naive thinking and an assumption that a restructure equals progress and changes in behaviour.

When growing – consider carefully the drive to add more roles and departments

When in the middle of growth, it can be hard for leaders to see the wood for the trees and challenge assumptions or positions. Clearly, growth may require the addition of a new function or bringing in some expertise. Marketing is a role not often found in a small not-for-profit, but can make the life of a CEO much more rewarding when he or she can call upon expertise readily to hand. Similarly, more people to deliver specific work or projects may be necessary as demand changes, perhaps suddenly.

However, as we seek to develop a culture of responsibility (and leaders who will step up to take responsibility and behave responsibly), we should use the thinking detailed earlier in this book to ask whether the enlargement of a department or team is truly needed, or whether it is pandering to an ego or self-promotional agenda. For example, when feeling exposed or vulnerable, a possible response is to appoint some leaders below oneself, both to protect and also to create the illusion of importance. It may be that increased complexity requires specialist support, but this does not always need to take the form of a fixed role. Responsible leaders see how to combine opportunities with needs. An imaginative solution might be to stretch or motivate an effective emerging leader or successful team with the opportunity to learn new knowledge and bring that to the table.

Restructuring to create the illusion of progress

Just as busyness can seem like effective progress, so too can restructuring organizations. I am not going to go into an analysis of the best structures for organizational effectiveness, for this has been written about extensively. Moreover, it is a very personal and local thing, for there is no one shape that fits all. What I do want to do is challenge us as leaders to consider what we expect a restructuring to do and how we can breathe life to a structure.

We have mentioned already that culture is shaped by behaviours, decisions and choices, often small but cumulatively comprising the way things are done around here. So when a business is constantly reviewing the value-add of support services functions, for example, and/or restructuring sales force teams to shelve costs, that itself will become part of the cultural norm. And it can be illusory, as it can mask avoidance issues. Faced with tough conversations to tackle an issue or opening up previously entrenched positions with new perspectives, many leaders will opt for a safer route that commissions a review or 'rearranges the chairs on the deck'. What is not often done to start with is to explore the behaviours that are being exhibited and those that are needed to enhance performance.

For example, an organization recognizes the need for a new area of expertise. A manager is brought on board who brings with him a small team from his previous employer. The function proves to add value in the immediate term. After a year or two, the function has grown and has created its own unique culture built around the original manager, who has now been promoted to a director level. It is widely known to be somewhat elitist in its approach to recruitment and development, preferring to keep things 'in house'. Other teams find it difficult to relate to the function, and meetings begin to be dominated by hidden agendas and posturing. Costs have come under review. In these situations, it is common for senior leaders to commission a review of the structure, hopeful that they can find cost savings. Heads can be taken out. Departments can be merged or outsourced. A new template can be imposed upon the business.

Unfortunately, the behaviours that have led to silo mindsets and building of empires may not have been addressed. Furthermore, an imposed new structure can create one of three emotional responses:

- curiosity, which leads to acceptance;
- ambivalence, which leads to inertia;
- insecurity, which leads to defensive responses.

In the case of the latter, in many respects this is helpful as it surfaces issues that can be tackled, if leadership appreciates its role in helping people deal with negative emotional responses. David Rock's work in this area is a valuable tool. His SCARF framework (Rock, 2008; Rock and Cox, 2012) identifies the fact that people's negative responses are triggered by threat to their perceived **status** or position in a hierarchy, their sense of **certainty**, the extent to which they feel their **autonomy** is diminished, how their sense of belonging and **relatedness** are likely to change, and how they perceive that **fairness** has been called into question. Rock contests that leaders should recognize that our brains are prediction machines and that we tend to read into situations things that may or may not be there. Once they understand this conceptually, leaders can take steps practically to engage with their people through dialogue to explore these reactions constructively. This is critical and an example of responsible leadership in action.

Interestingly, it can be the middle response of ambivalence that proves in the long run to be the least constructive. An ambivalent response is often borne out of experience that such reviews or restructures have happened regularly in the past and have not brought about any significant changes. Therefore, the most effective human response is to keep one's head down and wait for the merry-go-round to come round again. Such reactions are natural and are a form of passive defence. However, they reveal a culture where nobody is prepared to take responsibility for challenging assumptions or bringing new thinking that will truly equip the business to take on the future. What is fostered is a dullness and a lowering of expectation and ambition – hardly the stuff of high performance. This is a form of paralysis and delusion – expecting that doing more of the same will bring about change.

So how can we avoid this trap? Initially we should acknowledge that a structure chart is just that – a chart. It does not reflect how people behave and work together. It is words, roles and lines that illustrate a relationship or hierarchy. Metaphorically it is a skeleton and needs sinews, flesh, arteries, blood to flow, personality and character to bring it life. A responsible leader will pause to notice, think and explore before reacting, and especially to ask the questions that are uncomfortable, including:

- What are we avoiding by relying on a restructure to solve our problems?
- What behaviours are desirable and would remove the need to 'rearrange the chairs'?
- What have we tolerated or accepted as the norm that should be challenged before we jump into a full-scale restructuring?
- What as leaders have we failed to do before now that has contributed to where we are?
- How can we involve our people proactively in the discussions instead of imposing a new structure upon them?
- What if we did nothing to restructure but instead focused on the way we work together in the system?
- How will a restructure assist us to develop a culture of responsibility and enable us to respond better to the demands of the modern world?

Don't just promote the usual suspects

This is a simple point. In my work with senior people, helping them to understand their responsibility for managing their talent resources, one of the most difficult discussions is always around the difference between performance and potential. When thinking about building a culture of responsibility and an organization that will thrive in the modern world, it is important to ask the fundamental questions:

- Will what we have sought and valued in our leaders in the past still be the kinds of things that will be needed for the future?
- If not, what should we be looking for in our next generation of leaders?
- How can we identify this early enough?

In Part 1, we suggested some new paradigms and qualities that next-generation responsible leaders might demonstrate, and these can form a good starting point for the discussions. Nonetheless, we should not under-estimate the pressure to promote only top performers into key roles. After all, these are people who have delivered results and success thus far. The thinking follows that they will continue to deliver results in the future, irrespective of the conditions.

This may, of course, be true. However, it may also be a tough request of strong performers to ask them to adapt and behave differently to respond to new pressures in the system. Performance against objectives is one way of determining future effectiveness. Sadly, it can also be deceptive. Morgan McCall in his work on *High Flyers* (1998) points out that we should be mindful of how such talented people have succeeded and consider what the possible derailers for them might be once promoted. The following are examples to consider:

- They are strongly independent and do it all themselves – this may be found out when they have to lead other strong individuals and develop a team, and they may struggle to share the glory.
- They are (over) demanding of others and for a season this works – but they can burn people out regularly.
- They are frenetically energetic, which is infectious, and there is a real buzz around them – but they can sometimes fail to pause, reflect and learn.
- They are very competitive and attract winners – but they can be unable to deal with defeat and, at worst, resort to unfair tactics and short-term thinking.
- They are deep experts who have pushed the boundaries of thinking – but they can struggle when required to contribute strategically and think broadly, or build a team around them.

- They are known as highly effective networkers and relationship people, popular and liked by everyone – but they can fail to stand for anything and risk becoming all things to all men; will they challenge poor behaviour if need be?

- They are ambitious and have volunteered for numerous roles on high-profile projects – but they may be less willing to put in the hard work to deliver when circumstances are complex or against them.

What we need to do as leaders is to ensure that when thinking about promotions and key roles we are prepared to go beneath the surface and ask ourselves whether these strong performers do have what it takes to lead responsibly for the future. Remember, we are interested in the core as well as capabilities and evidence of performance. Through open-minded dialogue across the system we can review the usual suspects *and* look for unusual suspects coming from unlikely sources. HR and L&D departments have an important role to hold business leaders to account for the longer-term talent strategy and execution, not just the short term. This will include how senior leaders proactively coach and mentor newly appointed key individuals to enable great transitions.

Reflections

- How diverse is the talent pipeline in your organization?

- How can/do you define future potential in your organization?

- What alternative sources of key talent can you investigate to balance the traditional sources you use and help you develop a culture of responsibility?

- How are emerging talent and newly appointed leaders coached and mentored through transitions?

Measurement alone will not change behaviour

The old adage says that what gets measured gets done. But as we have seen, what gets done is not always what should be done if we are mindful of the wider responsible agenda. Simply measuring increased revenue and sales does not provide any comfort that customers have had their needs met fully or that ethical guidelines have been followed.

Barry Oshry's work on understanding systems (2007) identifies that leaders at the top of an organization have a tendency to ask for more and more information from their departments and business units to reassure themselves that progress is being made against goals and strategies. They believe that they have a need to be in control and, given a traditional reliance on data and evidence, they assume that the more information they have and the more often they have it, the more in control they feel. The impact that this has on people in the middle or at the bottom of the organizational system is almost inevitably not the impact that was intended.

A client of mine who works in a global software business is in charge of sales for a large region. He has recently taken up a new role, replacing his former boss, and is now in the unenviable position of being the 'top'. The previous boss apparently delighted in daily and weekly phone calls to his sales force to find out how the numbers were going. Quarterly targets drove the business activity, and regularly, as the end of the quarter approached, the sales force was required to focus on completing deals to meet a predetermined number.

To the extent that what gets measured gets done is true, this inevitably had the effect of generating anxiety about whether targets had been reached and, if not, how to tell a story to justify the position or what could be done quickly to rectify the situation. But is this the behaviour that is desired? Is it responsible behaviour? Does it foster a climate where people can be innovative and free to think beyond the obvious?

Another client – a partner in a large global professional services business – took on the role of leading a business unit, only to find that a large part of his time was being consumed by providing reports and information to what he described as 'the centre'. These requests were being driven from many different sources in 'the centre', each with legitimate reasons, having been asked to lead an initiative or effect a change. However, the combined impact of all these requests was to wear down the leader, and as there seemed to be no coherent pattern or prioritizing for these requests, he found he was responding to the latest request all the time. His frustration stemmed from his desire to become more proactive and strategic with his area of the business, but feeling that his energy was constantly being sucked out of him by requests from 'the centre'.

This describes a real conundrum for the responsible leader, namely how to remain on top of things and know what is going on while giving enough space for people to lead locally. It also challenges us to think about how we manage initiatives and change programmes in a more coherent way, so that the purpose and focus of activity are not diluted. And yet we know that the world is complex, with demands and pressures coming from all parts of our systems.

We need to return to some of the principles we discussed in Part 1. Leaders who are comfortable not knowing all the information free themselves to allow others to lead and innovate. Leaders who see the whole system and beyond the immediate are more able to flex their approach and cultivate a calmer mood. Leaders who engage person to person, leader to team, are able to listen and foster a climate where co-creation can happen.

When leaders or a 'centre' are requesting data in a frequent manner (over-frequent in some cases) without there being a clear benefit or communicated reason, there is a real risk of this turning into the worst form of measurement. Measurement becomes the goal in itself and roles are created to gather data and pass it on to more senior people. These roles can become institutionalized very quickly and even resented by the 'middles and bottoms' of the organization.

Where measurement apparently conflicts with passion

Just ask any teacher or doctor why they do what they do, and the response will include a significant element of conviction, vocation and passion. The same is probably true of actors, artists, scientists, chefs, church leaders, community workers – the list is extensive, as is to be hoped, given that we know how important passion is when operating in the flow. Nonetheless, the modern world wrestles with the need to justify cost and deliver value for money as we have accepted the many different stakeholder agendas at work in the system. To what extent are these mutually exclusive? Old thinking would suggest that they are. The argument goes: 'You cannot measure a nurse's care for a patient or a teacher's inspiration felt by a pupil.' This is true in part and also an example of limiting thinking.

Anthony runs a medium-sized business delivering care services in a local community. This includes running care homes for the elderly. His business is under scrutiny to deliver value for money and quality care. His workforce is struggling to come to terms with being more openly accountable for quality, and any talk of profit is treated with disdain. Anthony recognizes that his challenge as a responsible leader is to deflect attention from the measurement and refocus it on the fact that *because staff care and are passionate*, their values system drives them to pay attention when an elderly resident is vulnerable or to develop relationships with families that reassure them of the personal touch. **Performance flows from an attitude of responsibility built on passion.** Where it can go wrong is when the language, tone and frequency of measurement appear to say to the workforce that 'we do not trust you and we need to keep checking up on you', or 'what you are passionate about doing is not really what is important. It is the money that counts'. Such a mindset, whether justified or otherwise, will conflict with the drive for autonomy or mastery or purpose (Daniel Pink) and cause internal disease. It sows dissonance in the culture, and under such circumstances a worker can easily retreat to defensive or protective behaviours. **For the responsible leader, it becomes paramount that there is a clear narrative and link between outcomes and why and how they are being measured.** For the care home, it is because they care that levels of urinary tract infections are lower than elsewhere – and these are what are measured.

There is no easy remedy to the dilemma of 'to measure is to justify but also to inhibit'. However, some pragmatic guidance includes (reflect also on the extent to which you and your organization work like this):

- Keep measurements to the bare minimum but focused on what is truly important as genuine outcomes.

- Limit measuring inputs and activity as much as possible.

- Engage with stakeholder groups intentionally to clarify what it is that is really important to them and that could inform what and how performance is measured.

- Engage proactively with teams through generative dialogue to arrive at an agreed series of measures that work for everyone and that people understand *and* accept.

- Through this process, agree what is the ideal and most relevant frequency of measuring (asking for information) within the overriding principle that providing information takes time and energy, so a balance needs to be struck constructively.

- Inspire accountability rather than demand it through focusing on values, significance and passion for the work.

- Join up who is asking for information from around the organization and how often, so that deliverers of services remain free to operate.

Summary

In this chapter we have probed deeper into four areas where organizations can unintentionally trip up in their attempts to create a responsible culture. As is so often the case with leadership, it is an art form rather than a science per se. It involves dealing with volatile human beings, and in the modern complex and uncertain world, avoiding all pitfalls is going to prove very difficult. Nonetheless, forewarned is forearmed and we can be open to recognize some typical unintended consequences from our original good intentions:

- **Pitfall: just saying the words does not equal progress or change.** Response:
  - Get beneath the surface.
  - Avoid over-communication.
  - Properly align reward, recognition and performance management to responsibility.
- **Myth: restructuring alone will yield results.** Consider:
  - When growing, consider carefully the drive to add more roles and departments.
  - Restructures create either curiosity and acceptance but also ambivalence and inertia or insecurity.
  - Tackle behaviours before restructures.
- **Pitfall: don't just promote the usual suspects.** Response:
  - Create a diverse pipeline of talent.
  - Scan widely for potential emerging leaders.
  - Be aware of potential derailers.
- **Myth: measurement will change behaviour.** Consider:
  - Where measurement apparently conflicts with passion.
  - How to inspire accountability rather than demand it.
  - Link outcomes to the 'why' narrative.

In Part 2 we have looked into a possible organizational response to the need for responsible leadership by focusing on how organizations can develop responsible leaders and how the culture can facilitate this or inhibit it. These points are by no means the only organizational responses, and yet I do observe that inside the organizational system there is a tendency to over-engineer and over-complicate things. I have consulted with businesses that have inordinately complicated development frameworks and capability profiles for every role in the company. And when I ask managers and employees about these, and the extent to which they help enable performance, I am consistently met by blank faces and ambivalence. They level accusations about what these actually mean in practice, alongside the sense that the regulations have forced us into a corner around employment legislation, for example. Equally, I have seen gigantic succession planning processes supported by a multitude of spreadsheets. But when I have asked senior leaders if they actually know, and know thoroughly, their people and key talent in the pipeline, again the responses are patchy. Therefore, Part 2 has been something of a plea to simplify, to connect with what is essential and important, before embarking on processes and structures. It is about model-ling the thinking patterns and behavioural choices we have identified thus far in the book.

To practise something of what I have been talking about, in the final part of the book I want to paint a hopeful picture of how we are doing when it comes to responsible leadership in the early part of the 21st century and to surface a challenge for us all as individual leaders, wherever we are operating.

PART THREE
A visionary narrative

Our moments of truth

08

> *I am not bound to win but I am bound to be true. I am not bound to succeed but I am bound to live up to what light I have.* (ABRAHAM LINCOLN)

I began this book by suggesting that we are experiencing something of a revolution that could have an impact akin to that which the Industrial Revolution had in the 18th century. That period heralded the birth of the corporation, albeit via the route of the family-run industrial business. This new revolution is creating opportunities for individuals and communities to impact equally significantly and in so doing to challenge assumptions about success and effectiveness. It is something of a responsibility revolution, during which citizens are waking up to the realization that corporations and governments do not hold all the responsibility and answers. And so it is that, as with all revolutions, the old and the new coexist for a period, during which time tensions and conflicts surface, and ambiguity and complexity pervade our lives.

I want to suggest that as leaders we have the choice as to how we respond. The past decade has brought that choice into sharp relief, given that leadership has itself been under scrutiny following the corporate, religious and political exposés, principally around betrayal of trust and unethical behaviours. Not that leadership has avoided these kinds of issues in the past. All societies throughout history have wrestled with the tensions of leading in *their* moment with *their* peculiar circumstances for *their* times. And leaders have stepped forward with vision and purpose and integrity – famous and unknown alike; admired politicians, community and business leaders alongside the disliked and pilloried. Now is the moment of *our* choice.

We can choose to step forward to embrace the revolution and to harness its energy as forces for change for the greater good, or we can choose to resist by relying on old paradigms. Clearly, we also have the choice to use the revolutionary forces for narrow or harmful ends.

During this chapter, I will suggest something akin to a way of being for the responsible leader and summarize a responsible leadership response to these forces. Finally, I will remind us of some individuals and organizations that are carving out the path ahead for us.

A new way of being – stepping forward for the greater good

In Part 1 we identified fresh paradigms for responsible leaders who exude internal assuredness and attractiveness; adapt and are oriented to learn; think and operate relationally; inspire others with purpose and focus. We explored how this new (perhaps rediscovered) mode of leading thinks systemically by balancing self, organizational and wider-world demands, and makes sense of key paradoxes in our world to listen through the noise, see beyond the immediate and consider how to redefine success.

In Part 2 we focused more on how the organization can create the conditions for development, learning and a culture to evolve that facilitates responsible leadership behaviours.

This chapter will suggest that to bind these ingredients together requires a fundamental way of being that is going to come more to the fore if we are to make this revolution one that future generations will look back on appreciatively. That is, **an orientation towards a greater good – bigger than the individual on his or her own or the corporation on its own**; bigger even than a nation focused on its own advantage over others.

The greater good can mean many things to different people, and it is potentially nebulous as a concept. However, we have to start from a basis of some kind. Either we believe it is possible to benefit many and for many to prosper based on how we co-create and collaborate, or we are thrown back on to the altar of local advantage over one another that leads to a continual striving for dominance through protectionism and defensive behaviours.

Let us not be deceived: this is not an easy path to take. It will require those that choose it to tap into an aspect of human nature that many have subordinated to their goals of success. To be contributing for the greater good requires us to be 'otherish', as Adam Grant puts it and as we explored earlier. That is, to be interested in giving rather than taking, to be generous of spirit rather than protectionist. The good news is that the revolution is raising up people who are choosing this route. These are people who have chosen to step forward and to think, based on hope, that they can and should make a contribution. **This is the second aspect of the new way of being – 'I can and I will' as a response.**

This can seem at odds with a pervading 20th-century paradigm in which we are encouraged to assume that someone else will do it or someone else is to blame. We are conditioned to respond with *'they should; they must; you need to'*. Collectively we begin to understand at a deeper level that *'we should; we need to'*, but this still leaves a response as external rather than internally owned. We have reached this point unconsciously for most of us, through: increased reliance on centralized provision of services, for example health and education; over-centralized government and regulation that looks to control behaviour; corporations that direct our needs and wants through advertising; and education systems that focus more on advantage and consumerism rather than citizenship. For example, perversely, governments now have to legislate to encourage whistleblowers in the public and private sectors to step forward, for fear of recriminations in the workplace.

How can we help ourselves cultivate this different way of being?

By paying attention to where it is evident. It is a simple message, but we can use the enhanced learning cycle we introduced in Part 2 as a guide. Once we begin to investigate stories of this new approach or put ourselves in places and situations in which responsible leadership is being modelled, we can begin to make sense of our own emotional responses and choices. Clearly, this requires us to be open rather than closed to seeing, listening, noticing – to be oriented to learn.

Fortunately, the revolution is helping us in this regard. Through social media platforms we are now able to follow real examples as they unfold. News coverage reaches the farthest parts of the globe to bring us coverage of the bad and the good, the sad and the uplifting. **We can harness the technological revolution as a force for good to share positive examples of responsible leadership in action.** For example, Cancer Research UK (a major charity in the UK focused on developing a cure for all cancers) found itself £8 million better off within six days as a result of the 'no makeup selfie' campaign in which the famous and not so famous (mostly women) took photos of themselves without their makeup and posted these to raise money for the cause. The charity did not start the campaign, an individual did. Another case includes a viral campaign that encourages people to throw a bucket of ice-cold water over themselves, to post the video online and donate to a cause and to nominate others to follow suit, in this case motor neurone disease. Such is the power of this way of communicating that former presidents have been encouraged to participate. Consider the impact that can be achieved by visionary people focusing on responsible and positive acts rather than our tendency to want to read about negative and sensational news.

Another story to illustrate the point involves someone who has become a friend of mine. I met Cally while on a business trip to Brazil, having been given her contact details by a friend. I was interested in finding out more about life in Brazil on the ground. Over lunch she told me her story. Cally is a British woman who, during a time of personal anguish, found herself watching a news item about the plight of street children in São Paolo, Brazil. She was personally impacted and decided that something should be done about this and that she could respond. Unable to speak Portuguese and never having been to Brazil, she flew to São Paolo with the intention of doing something, perhaps naively, to fix the problem. She was met with the magnitude of the problem and soon realized that stepping forward to respond would be costly. Undaunted, a few years later she now runs the Eagle Project with her Brazilian husband George, based in São Paolo. They focus on working with incarcerated young offenders to help them work through their story via drama therapy. They are encouraged to explore their crimes from all angles, including the victim's perspective, and to build some personal restoration amid the trauma that their young lives have been through. She now speaks fluent Portuguese and has changed the lives of many young men and women, giving them a sense of purpose against a backdrop of nihilism. Having visited the maximum-security youth prison in São Paolo to witness their work, it is both humbling and challenging.

Cally and George's story is one of thousands around the world where individuals have been inspired to respond with 'I can and I will'. The global charity TearFund, in partnership with Tear (Netherlands), has brought some of these together under the umbrella of 'Inspired Individuals' – a project that seeks to build a global community of learning and action by bringing together individuals from developing lands around the world to encourage them to scale up their initial local ideas and make inroads into significant social issues. To read their website and the stories of Inspired Individuals is to be inspired oneself (see later list of organizations). What is worth noticing is how Gary Swart – Executive Director of 'Inspired Individuals' – and his team saw beyond the provision of aid and support to alleviate poverty (one of the principal aims of TearFund) to come alongside people who themselves had already stepped forward with an idea and were implementing it in their own backyard. Their formula of the right person with the right idea in the right place at the right time, who is then given nurturing support from a team of coaches and experts, is founded on the belief of creating a sustainable initiative and spreading expertise as people take up personal responsibility. The Inspired Individuals are themselves required to generate funding and provided with only a small grant from the charity to avoid creating dependency. It is collaboration and co-creation in action for the greater good.

Perhaps one of the more famous examples of this principle at work is the Grameen Bank founded by Muhammad Yunus in Bangladesh in 1976. Long before responsibility and sustainability became a popular vogue, Muhammad Yunus tapped into something local and met a need for micro finance for the poorest of the community as a way of raising their aspirations and living standards. Yunus challenged assumptions about financial loans to the poor by building on what he noticed, namely that women were more responsible than men in that community and were passionate about providing for their families and communities, through demonstrating that collaboration was possible. His micro loans of a few hundred pounds provided the seed capital for women to start small enterprises and raise living standards. Moreover, repayment rates are in excess of 90 per cent, which is remarkable in the financial services world. His borrowers own 90 per cent of the business, which clearly encourages them to want it to thrive. Grameen is no small operation. There are over 7 million active clients and the bank is a multi-billion-dollar operation. Yunus relies on trust and core values that support mutual benefit – the greater good. He was awarded the Nobel Peace Prize in 2006 and over the subsequent years the world has seen an explosion of micro finance and credit unions in developing *and* developed economies. How this movement continues to grow in influence is worth observing closely, for it represents an optimistic response to the mistrust and profiteering so evident in the mainstream banking sector.

Earlier we said that we could put ourselves in places and situations to experience responsible leadership in action. **We proposed using immersion learning as a way to do this for organizations, and the good news is that the generational forces operating in the revolution are also helping us.** Nowadays, as emerging generations enter the workforce, it is common for many of them to have spent time travelling or working in imaginative organizations and places. Such experiences serve to widen perspectives and reveal the interconnectedness of our global village. Furthermore, as career patterns evolve, organizations can look for ways to harness the regenerative aspects of career breaks or sabbaticals from which individuals benefit. Leaders of larger organizations can avoid feeling threatened and inconvenienced by changing work patterns by embracing them wholeheartedly. If employee engagement is an important goal for businesses, then enlightened engagement strategies include the importance of recognizing personal life goals and development as a means to fulfilment.

I recently came across a new enterprise that provides opportunities for young graduates and other volunteers to join short-term assignment teams that help local communities, in developing economies, develop local businesses. What caught my attention was that this was born out of a desire felt by two recent graduates – Joshua Bicknall and Douglas Cochrane – to do something valuable and meaningful, given that they were unable to secure 'normal jobs' in their home country. And so Balloon Ventures was formed, bringing men and women with experience of commercial businesses alongside enthusiastic graduates to build immersion-learning experiences that create employment in developing economies. Through a systemic lens the leverage this creates is huge. These young volunteers will return to their homelands with a responsible leadership mindset and some of the skills necessary to envision others. Moreover, it is to be hoped that they will themselves develop into responsible leaders of others.

Future generations demand that the older generations respond constructively to the resource crisis and environmental agenda. Excessive consumption attracts negative publicity, and again technology can help us. In my work as an executive coach, it is now possible for me to see and speak to a client in another part of the world or time zone, using video conferencing, which has come a long way since I first encountered it 20 years ago. No longer do all meetings have to happen where we can actually shake hands, and this saves time and fuel resources. Granted, at the present moment, it seems that nothing can replace the connection that comes through touch and feeling someone's presence, but it would be a brave person who would limit thinking to say that technology will one day somehow enable this to happen remotely.

Big business is playing its part, as we have already seen with the M&S 'Plan A' agenda. My former employer PwC recently commissioned a new head office building in London which is carbon-neutral even to the extent of reusing chip fat as one aspect of the fuel mix. Again, though, we can also notice where less lauded examples are happening and pointing the way, for it is how we individually model 'I can and I will' that collectively will add up to real change. Lambourne End Centre for Outdoor Learning, which we encountered earlier, is one place that seeks to educate young people from disadvantaged backgrounds and inner-city London about the value of organic husbandry, introducing them to the realities of looking after animals and recycling waste.

The rise of social enterprise

Corporations that emerged during and after the Industrial Revolution have been the key driver of wealth creation over the centuries since, and have birthed remarkable innovations across all aspects of our lives. However, it is now apparent that societies are waking up to the fact that these entities are not the only way to innovate, to provide services and do business. Likewise, large-scale public sector providers are being invited to reassess how they too can reinvent themselves and become more agile. Health, education, waste disposal and care for the elderly are all areas where communities are acknowledging their responsibility to shape and own the future.

An important aspect of this shift is the rise of the social enterprise and community-interest companies that embody greater local accountability and typically reinvest profits into the work itself rather than provide returns to potentially anonymous shareholders. The value of these organizations is in their ability to be flexible and to innovate quickly, unburdened by large infrastructure and overheads. Moreover, in the vacuum of trust and respect created by the various scandals we have already mentioned, the general public have become suspicious of large-scale business, preferring the values and apparent trustworthiness of enterprises to which they can relate more closely.

Access to capital to finance growth or expansion will be an issue for this type of business, but again the forces at work in the revolution have begun to offer answers through crowd sourcing, where social media is used to generate investments. Enterprises that are distrustful of banks as a typical source of capital have used the company limited-edition bonds route, again tapping into a groundswell of stakeholder involvement in ownership.

Whether and how this third sector continues to grow in influence is unclear. No doubt there will be failures that will be reported along the way. But important influential bodies such as the RSA in the UK and leading global business schools are now devoting serious energy to researching this sector and its future contribution to a remodelled economy in which coexistence of differing types of enterprise is the norm. Enlightened mainstream corporations have already begun to sponsor a kind of collaboration, as we saw earlier with the M&S case study and the Oasis case study. Governments likewise are courting social entrepreneurs (as well as mainstream business entrepreneurs and leaders) to help them devise policies that connect with communities and wider society, and use cheaper delivery models for services.

I do not intend to open up a political debate, but it does seem increasingly clear that the new order is one in which central control and regulation are going to be at odds with the groundswell of agile innovation and creativity beginning to burst through the surface. If this is true, responsible political leaders will be those that can create climates that enable, release and then carefully harness rather than restrict and control. Let us not kid ourselves, either: this will present major crises of conscience and ideology, which for many will be alien and uncomfortable.

If this route encourages more citizenship and taking up of responsibility, it will play a major part in reshaping the next few decades in which what were thought of as normal rules may not necessarily apply and new ways of being will emerge.

Learning from and becoming alchemists

Providing a precise definition of responsible leadership and a responsible leader is fraught with danger in such volatile times, but I believe it to embrace the work of William R Torbert and David Rooke in their study on leadership transformations (2005). Their findings reveal seven action logics (leaders' interpretations of their worlds and their corresponding actions): Opportunist, Diplomat, Expert, Achiever, Individualist, Strategist and Alchemist. According to Torbert and Rooke, it is important to develop leaders through these levels, as each one is more or less effective given specific circumstances and conditions. For example, we can see that experts (interestingly, the largest reporting category of leader – 38 per cent) are hugely effective in the know-ledge economy and the professional services or financial services economies, as they seek to lead by influencing based on knowledge.

In our study of responsible leadership, it is the latter two categories that require our attention and, not surprisingly, these represent a very small per-centage of those surveyed – 4 and 1 per cent, respectively. **Strategists** are concerned with transformation and change at a personal and an organiza-tional level through creating visions that bind together people across all the different 'action logics', as Torbert and Rooke put it:

> According to the Strategist's action logic, organizational and social change is an iterative development process that requires awareness and close leadership attention.
>
> Achievers will use their influence to successfully promote their own companies. The Strategist works to create ethical principles and practices beyond the interests of herself or her organization.

In our words, they see beyond and see the value of studying the inter-connectedness in the system, and they see the greater good as an objective.

Alchemists, according to Torbert and Rooke, generate movements for social transformation, integrating material, spiritual and societal factors. Such individuals are rare, as they seem to be able to operate effectively at a macro and micro level:

> He can talk to both kings and commoners. He can deal with immediate priorities yet never lose sight of long-term goals.

Torbert and Rooke identify that these individuals seek out and focus on truth. They notice the moment of truth, in history, for themselves and their organization, speaking to people's hearts and minds to mobilize response.

Historically, leaders with Alchemist characteristics have included shapers such as Martin Luther King Jnr, Gandhi and Nelson Mandela, all of whom had an ability to identify truth amid the noise of their turbulent times and to find ways first to model it themselves and then to capture others' emotional connection at the soul and heart level.

Business leaders with these characteristics are perhaps less celebrated. One could argue that the early Quakers were Alchemists in their approach to business and building communities, with ways of life that were manifestly different from previously. To bring this up to the current day, Paul Polman of Unilever is striking out with a leadership authority that seems to straddle the Strategist and Alchemist. In an article entitled 'Interview: Unilever's Paul Polman on diversity, purpose and profits' published in the *Guardian* on 2 October 2013, Jo Confino reported Paul Polman's views on authenticity, transparency, a sense of purpose in business and why profit warnings don't worry him.

His vision to transform his business by growing it in new markets in ethical, sustainable and responsible ways is clearly one for our times. Moreover, he recognizes that his business is uniquely placed to do this, as it provides basic products for human well-being and as such can transform the lives of millions across the world. Critically, he has commissioned social audits of the Unilever supply chain in all its markets, as he recognizes that being responsible means taking end-to-end responsibility (not just talking about it). He is concerned with the long game for Unilever and the sustainability of the planet – Project Sunlight, which we highlighted in Chapter 6 – *and* he is aware of the reality of running a corporation that has more short-term accountabilities. But as we discussed previously, he is not afraid to buck the trend and openly put less value on short-term reporting that is just to please the stock markets.

Whether Polman's courageous stance creates the organizational and societal changes he envisions (together with many others), time will tell. What is clear is that he is stepping forward and responding with 'I can and I will' because 'I feel compelled to' – for the greater good, including, of course, his business – Unilever.

The question now, however, is 'how can each of us become more of an Alchemist leader locally in our organizations and in our communities?' We can call on the leaders of large multinationals or wealthy philanthropists such as Bill Gates to create movements of change, as they have the resources so to do. But if we have learnt anything from exploring responsible leadership and the times we live in, it is surely that we too can step forward and notice the truth amid the noise, and respond with 'I can and I will'. Our responsibility is to look for those who are demonstrating more 'otherish', togetherness, collaboration, a spirit of co-creation, optimism, generosity and care for stewardship, and to learn from them – to work with them. Equally, it is to become those people who attract people around them to collectively respond to moments of truth, however big or small, however short term or long term.

Social movements are being born more frequently now than ever before. YouTube, Facebook, Twitter and Google have all changed the world over the past ten years. And yet, as Steve Chalke reminded us, people still want leaders who they can trust, who they can relate to, who understand them and their worlds, and who take responsibility for their actions and choices.

This vision is about educating and stretching ourselves as leaders and the next generations to look for where there is optimism and hope and to find ways to learn and build for the greater good. Many businesses are trying to do this and making progress. They will fail in part, but we should be slow to judge and quick to encourage. This journey is one of discovery for us and will be rocky and unclear at times. Leaders will find resistance from people who don't get it, but can draw on the encouragement from the movement that is happening more widely now. After all, who else is there to lead the revolution, if not us?

Organizations and places to look for responsible leadership at work

Over the years of working in this area, I have gathered examples of people and organizations that inspire me. I have introduced some of these during the book to illustrate key aspects of responsible leadership in action. What I have also come to realize is that no one organization can say that it is fully modelling responsible leadership. That would be an absurd claim, given that we are in the midst of a revolution and a process of discovery of what forms this might take in reality. However, there are places inside large and small organizations alike where inspired people are working together to demonstrate a more responsible approach. In time, the hope is that these will infect more of the organizations and cause senior leaders to join up and align the parts of their enterprises behind the common responsible narrative.

I share a few of these with you now, simply by way of encouragement. There are many, many more, if you look around you. Part of our role as more responsible leaders is to scan more widely, to investigate where we see something that looks to be modelling responsible leadership and to support, perhaps by buying products or giving encouraging feedback to leaders who have stepped forward courageously.

Social enterprises/charities

- *Columba 1400*: a centre for developing leaders, bringing business leaders and groups of underprivileged young people together to inspire vision;
- *Balloon Ventures*: providing short-term immersion learning experiences in developing economies;
- *Common Purpose*: bringing leaders from around the world and across communities to explore collaboration in action;
- *Eden Project*: educating generations about sustainable living;
- *Oasis*: building communities through holistic education, health and well-being;
- *Tearfund*: inspiring local individuals as part of their international relief work;
- *Belu Water*: a 100 per cent carbon-neutral company that gives its profits to WaterAid, a charity dedicated to improving the supply of clean water to the developing world;
- *Abundant Community*: Peter Block's initiative to encourage local communities to draw more deeply on their own resources and resourcefulness.

Businesses that are trying hard, doing their best and some great work

These are a few examples of the kind of optimism that is building if we care to look broadly:

- *Unilever*: looking to integrate its supply chain and lead responsibly in diverse territories around the world; provoking wider stakeholder involvement through the Project Sunlight initiative;

- *PwC*: using experiential immersion learning to develop a cadre of responsible leaders who will themselves influence wider companies as advisers; supporting social enterprises with resources and mentoring;

- *M&S*: aiming to be the world's premier sustainable retailer through the Plan A initiative;

- *Starbucks*: developing youth leaders; connecting store managers with coffee providers using immersion experiences;

- *Body Shop*: continuing the legacy of Dame Anita Roddick by championing fair trade alongside other causes that support diversity;

- *HSBC*: partnering with Earthwatch, WaterAid and World Wildlife Fund to develop strategies to manage water provision more effectively and educate communities;

- *Google*: among many initiatives, it supports Citizen Schools in North America and encourages volunteers to play an active part in the education of young people, especially in science, technology, engineering and mathematics;

- *Coca-Cola*: the global behemoth seeking to empower 5 million women by 2020 through partnering with different stakeholders in the wider system and across many different countries;

- *Patagonia*: a company that makes outdoor clothing and equipment, persuading through its energetic and passionate founder Yvon Chouinard large retailers such as Walmart and Nike to embrace a sustainable and environmental agenda through the Sustainable Apparel Coalition;

- *Grameen Group*: leading the way with micro credit to raise the poorest of the world out of poverty through enterprise;

- *The John Lewis Partnership*: championing employee engagement through willing buy-in to an inspiring and shared vision; promoting fairer supplier and customer policies;

- *Innocent*: an innovative drinks and healthy food company overtly donating 10 per cent of profits to enterprise initiatives in the developing world; winning wider stakeholder engagement to an imaginative vision;

- *Pret a Manger*: a fast-food business with a difference, using locally sourced produce in its products; supporting homeless charities through its community foundation;

- *Leadership Trust*: providing leadership development focusing on authenticity; based in a location that uses local natural resources and recycles water to prove that sustainability does not have to be the domain of large organizations;

- *Ashridge Business School*: one of the leading global business schools offering leading-edge programmes in sustainability and leading responsibly;

- *Winchester Business School*: a small niche business school encouraging the responsible leadership debate through the Hoare Centre for Responsible Leadership based at Winchester;

- *RSA*: The Royal Society for encouragement of Arts, Manufactures and Commerce (based in London), which has championed innovative thinking for centuries and now leads the debate on new models for communities, social enterprise, political, economic and social thinking for the 21st century.

Conclusion

We began with a picture of leadership in something of a crisis of trust and respect. Business and political leaders have lost their way in the eyes of the public. Followers, citizens and consumers alike are demanding greater accountability.

As with any wake-up call, there will be those whose ears are closed and who will fail to respond. And, reassuringly, there will be those who heed the call. This book is for them. It is one small offering in that call, and throughout I have sought to encourage and offer simple ways forward. To be a responsible leader is not easy in the face of the storm of conflicting forces, including human nature in all its forms. However, it is as necessary as a captain's firm hand on the tiller of a yacht in the storm, or the navigator's calm assurance of a course through the treacherous rocks. To be a responsible leader is to step forward into the space and the moment with an 'I can and I will' mindset to impact situations and systems for the greater good. At times we will need to hold fast and at other times it will require a more gentle guiding hand. What I have seen first hand, however, is that to be a responsible leader is hugely rewarding, fulfilling and highly attractive. And in this, there is hope.

Throughout this book there have been moments for you to reflect. I hope that you have been able to take the opportunity to do so and have begun to form your own views about being a responsible leader in *your* situation. As someone who is focused on provoking learning, I will finish with some final and simple reflections that will act as a launch pad for the next phase of your responsible leadership journey:

Reflections

- What are the ingredients of *your* personal responsible leadership narrative and with whom can you and will you share it *and* work it out?

- What will be happening around you when *you* are leading more responsibly?

- How can you start or work with a movement for responsibility in your situation?

REFERENCES

Boyatzis, R E and McKee, A (2005) *Resonant Leadership*, Harvard Business School Press, Boston, MA

Buckingham, M and Clifton, D (2004) *Now, Discover Your Strengths*, Simon & Schuster, London

Cadbury, D (2010) *Chocolate Wars*, Harper Press, London

Chalke, S and Blair, C (2009) *Stop the Traffik*, Lion Hudson plc, Oxford

Collins, J (2001) *Good to Great*, Random House Business, London

Collins, J (2009) *How the Mighty Fall*, HarperCollins, New York

Covey, S (1992) *The Seven Habits of Highly Effective People*, Simon & Schuster, London

Csíkszentmihályi, M (2002) *Flow: How to achieve happiness*, Random House, London

Denning, S (2011) *The Leader's Guide to Storytelling: Mastering the art and discipline of business narrative*, Jossey-Bass, San Francisco

Goffee, R and Jones, G (2006) *Why Should Anyone Be Led by You?* Harvard Business School Press, Boston, MA

Goleman, D (1996) *Emotional Intelligence: Why it can matter more than IQ*, Bloomsbury, London

Goleman, D (2013) *Focus: The hidden driver of excellence*, HarperCollins, New York

Gore, A (2006) *An Inconvenient Truth: The planetary emergency of global warming and what we can do about it*, Rodale Press, New York

Grant, A (2013) *Give and Take*, Weidenfeld & Nicolson, London

Greenleaf, R K (1998) *The Power of Servant Leadership*, Berrett-Koehler, San Francisco

Handy, C (2002) *The Empty Raincoat*, Arrow Books, London

Hersey, P and Blanchard, K H (1969) *Management of Organizational Behavior: Utilizing human resources*, Prentice Hall, NJ

Honey, P and Mumford, A (2006) *The Learning Styles Questionnaire: 80 item version*, Peter Honey Publications, Maidenhead

Kline, N (1999) *Time to Think*, Ward Lock, London

McCall, M (1998) *High Flyers: Developing the next generation of leaders*, Harvard Business School Press, Boston, MA

McKnight, J and Block, P (2010) *The Abundant Community: Awakening the power of families and neighborhoods*, Berrett-Koehler, San Francisco

Marks & Spencer [accessed 30 July 2014] Plan A Report 2007, *Marks and Spencer Group plc* [Online] http://corporate.marksandspencer.com/plan-a/ b6867fa1340d482da1ebde62c099dd69

Marks & Spencer and Accenture (2013) *Fortune Favours the Brave*, Marks & Spencer Group plc, London

Michaels, E, Handfield-Jones, H and Axelrod, B (1997) *The War for Talent*, Harvard Business School Press, Boston, MA

Middleton, J (2007) *Beyond Authority: Leadership in a changing world*, Palgrave Macmillan, Basingstoke

Oshry, B (2007) *Seeing Systems: Unlocking the mysteries of organizational life*, Berrett-Koehler, San Francisco

Piketty, T (2014) *Capital in the Twenty-First Century*, Belknap Press, Cambridge, MA

Pink, D (2009) *Drive: The surprising truth about what motivates us*, Riverhead Books, New York

Robinson, K (2009) *The Element: How finding your passion changes everything*, Penguin Group, New York

Rock, D (2008) SCARF: A brain-based model for collaborating with and influencing others, *NeuroLeadership Journal*, 1, pp 44–52

Rock, D and Cox, C (2012) SCARF in 2012: updating the social neuroscience of collaborating with others, *NeuroLeadership Journal*, 4, pp 1–14

Roddick, A (1992) *Body and Soul*, Vermilion, London

Rooke, D and Torbert, W (2005) Seven transformations of leadership, *Harvard Business Review*, **April**, pp 66–76

Steare, R (2009) *Ethicability: How to decide what's right and find the courage to do it*, Roger Steare Consulting Limited, London

Visser, W (2011) *The Age of Responsibility*, John Wiley & Sons, Chichester

INDEX